Beginner's Guide to Converted Coaches

Larry Plachno

Beginner's Guide to Converted Coaches

by Larry Plachno

For information write to:

Transportation Trails
9698 West Judson Road
Polo, Illinois 61064
Phone: (815) 946-2341

First Printing: February, 1992
Second Printing: February, 1994
Manufactured in the United States of America

Library of Congress Cataloging in Publication Data

Plachno, Larry, 1943-
  Beginner's guide to converted coaches / Larry Plachno.
  p.   cm.
  ISBN 0-933449-13-5
  1. Converted coaches.   I. Title.
  TL298.P63 1992
  629.226--dc20   91-45587
                                                       CIP

Publisher's Credits

Technical Proofreader: Michael P. Gallagher.

In-House Proofreaders: Jeff Robertson and Marion Harris.

Electronic Typesetting and Page Layout: National Bus Trader, Inc., Polo, Illinois.

Interior and Wiring Diagrams: Deb Barron, National Bus Trader, Inc., Polo, Illinois.

Printing and Binding: Rochelle Printing Co., Rochelle, Illinois.

Other Books by Larry Plachno

Sunset Lines
The Story of the Chicago Aurora & Elgin Railroad
1 — Trackage
(1986)

Sunset Lines
The Story of the Chicago Aurora & Elgin Railroad
2 — History
(1989)

The Longest Interurban Charter
(1988)

Used Intercity Bus Pricing 1978-1986
(1987)

The Beginner's Guide to Converted Coaches
is dedicated to

Kirwan M. Elmers

of Custom Coach Corporation
in Columbus, Ohio,
who, along with his father,
expanded an early concept by the Flxible Company
in converted coach interiors
and created the
converted coach industry
that we know today.

Cover Photo

MCI 102C3 converted by Custom Coach Corp. with a Landcruiser® interior. © 1991 HIGH TIDES PHOTOGRAPHY/CUSTOM COACH CORP.

Table of Contents

Interior of a Prevost coach converted by Custom Coach Corp. looking from the front lounge towards the rear. Noteworthy features include the angled galley area with European features, the side aisle design and the decorator-type shadow box in place of a dining area. © HIGH TIDES PHOTOGRAPHY/CUSTOM COACH CORP.

Foreword

When Larry Plachno asked me to look over the manuscript for this book, I really did not know what to expect. In the last few years I have read hundreds of articles on various subjects pertaining to converted coaches. No one, to my knowledge, has ever tried to cover the whole subject in a book written for the new or prospective owner. In writing a *Beginner's Guide to Converted Coaches*, Larry has done just that.

As a member of the Converted Coach Owners Club (an independent club where ownership of a converted coach is a requirement for membership), I have met many new owners. They usually ask the same questions about the same topics. Unfortunately, I usually do not get to meet them until after they have bought a coach. By then the answers to these questions can be a little late.

Driving a coach on the interstate highway system is not that much different than driving a large motorhome. With some practice it can be mastered by most. The new owner will soon realize that the ownership and upkeep of a converted coach *is* quite different from that of a motorhome. This book makes the prospective owner aware of these differences and helps them prepare for the needed changes. It also answers all of the commonly asked questions and some that should be asked.

The author covers the financial side of coach converting in an easy to understand manner. Instead of using dollar figures (which might not apply to all conversions), he uses the value of the shell as a percentage of the total cost of the conversion. This should help answer the all-important questions of "how much coach can we afford?" and "is it a good investment?"

I can only think how helpful this book would have been in my own case, years ago, when I first contracted "converted coach fever."

Not knowing any coach owners, I did not have any experience with coaches. After reading everything I could find in *Family Motor Coaching* magazine, I sent for every available back issue of *National Bus Trader*. I then spent months absorbing this material. Now I thought I was pretty well versed on the subject of coaches. Armed with all this new knowledge, I felt I was ready to go out and make an intelligent purchase. I then proceeded to go out and buy one of the first coaches I could find, paying 50% more than I thought I could afford and at least twice what the coach was worth. After six weeks of minor problems, the engine blew up. Being poorer but not much smarter, I had the engine rebuilt at the local truck garage. This cost about as much as a brand new motor and a trip to Hawaii for two! It seems they had never worked on a coach before and have not since.

If this book had been available back then, I might have done things differently. Of course without my expensive education in "how not to buy a converted coach," I might not have been asked to write this foreword.

I think Larry did a great job writing this book and I am hoping this will be the first in a long and successful series. Keep on coachin'.

Mike Gallagher
President,
Converted Coach Owners
October, 1991

Introduction

As recently as three decades ago, the private railroad car represented the ultimate in practical transportation luxury by providing a combination of convenient access to many destinations with the comforts of home. With the decline of the passenger train, the private railroad car has gone the route of the yacht in retaining its comforts but having very limited destination possibilities. Aviation failed to fill this gap. Although undeniably the fastest means of transport, the airplane is limited both by destination and by the comforts and amenities possible.

The new leader in the field of practical luxury transportation is the private motorcoach. It not only can travel virtually anywhere reached by an automobile but it can simultaneously provide all the comforts of home. Effectively a merger of the commercial intercity motorcoach with the RV concept, the private motorcoach offers the strength and durability of a commercial intercity bus combined with a customized interior.

The concept was first attempted commercially by the Flxible Company of Loudonville, Ohio in the late 1940s. A few years later, the operation was taken over by the Elmers family, moved to Columbus, and renamed Custom Coach Corp. It has subsequently fluorished and today is the most respected name in the conversion industry. In addition, the original concept has grown into a small industry. In 1991, there were several thousand private coaches on the highways in the United States and Canada.

Owners of private coaches are in good company. John Madden regularly travels by converted coach and many, if not most, of the leading country and western entertainers own or travel in converted coaches. The more expensive new units being turned out today carry a price tag in excess of $650,000. In spite of this, ownership of converted coaches is not necessarily limited to the very rich as is private railroad cars. Although retired couples predominate, many younger couples — including those with several children — enjoy the convenience and ambiance of a private coach. Initial investment can often be matched to individual financial requirements. Many owners report that actual out-of-pocket operating costs are less than the cost of operating a private automobile and staying at motels.

It would be a bad week here at the office of *National Bus Trader* magazine if we did not receive several phone calls from prospective private motorcoach owners seeking various types of information on the subject. We try our best to answer all of them and although many can be answered with an article from a back issue of *National Bus Trader,* others require a lengthy verbal reply.

Realizing that there is no other practical source for this information, we decided to put this little book together. It is designed primarily to answer the most often asked questions of the prospective or novice private coach owner. It is intentionally over simplistic so as to either pave the way for or to ease the transition to private motorcoach ownership and operation. We have intentionally refrained from going into more detailed information in this book for two reasons. The first is that it could be both confusing to the novice and more information than desired for an initial step. The second is that if this basic book is well received, our intention would be to invite or collaborate with converted coach experts to publish additional volumes on specific topics and thereby create the equivalent of a converted coach encyclopedia.

It should be mentioned that some of the material in this book is influenced by my own unusual entry into private coach ownership. I purchased my first bus at the age of 19 back in 1963 and subsequently spent several years in the commercial bus business as an employee, owner and consultant. When I made the transition to converted coaches, I was familiar with intercity coaches and their systems but had to learn the ''house'' or conversion systems. This is just the opposite of most newcomers to converted coaches who generally have prior RV experience and have to learn about coaches. However, this is most likely a positive thing since I feel that most private coach owners would be well advised to take a more professional attitude toward both the operation and maintenance of their vehicles.

I should apologize in advance for my over simplistic treatment of some subjects and curt observations found in the following pages. Much of this is the result of my nearly 30 years experience with buses coupled with a need to provide a relatively comprehensive overview of converted coaches in a short space for readers who presumably have little prior involvement. Hopefully, the future will permit us to provide more comprehensive volumes on individual topics.

I would be remiss if I did not acknowledge the kind assistance of Mike Gallagher, president of the Converted Coach Owners. Mike graciously reviewed the original manuscript for this book and made numerous suggestions and comments, most of which were incorporated into the final text.

Many of the more active private coach owners are subscribers to *National Bus Trader* which covers both private and commercial intercity coaches. It offers listings of used commercial and converted coaches for sale, a bi-monthly listing of used coach prices, information on suppliers, and frequent articles of interest to private coach owners. A free sample copy may be obtained by writing to: National Bus Trader, 9698 W. Judson Road, Polo, Illinois 61064 or by phoning (815) 946-2341.

For the record, my own current coach is an MC-8 that was converted new by Custom Coach Corp. of Columbus, Ohio. Being a second owner gave me a professionally converted coach with low mileage at a reasonable price. Since I travel a great deal, I often find myself on the road in all seasons, in all types of weather and usually turn about 20,000 miles annually, more than the average private coach owner. Like many converted coach owners, I find that much of my travels would be more difficult and certainly less comfortable if I had to do it any other way.

Larry Plachno
Polo, Illinois
October 18, 1991

1

Picking a Coach and Conversion Method

Once you have elected to become a converted coach owner you have several decisions in front of you. The most important of these is to select a coach and conversion method. For all practical purposes a converted coach can be described as a merger of two different things. One is the coach itself which is often called a shell when it has no interior or is referred to separately from the interior. The second is the interior and systems, often referred to simply as the conversion. Systems pertaining to the coach are referred to as coach systems and those pertaining to the conversion are called house systems. It is the proper and professional assembly and integration of these components and systems that makes a good converted coach.

Although there are some obvious alternatives, the acquisition of most converted coaches usually falls into one of three standard categories: 1) purchasing a new coach and having it professionally converted, 2) purchasing a used professionally converted coach, and 3) purchasing a used coach from a commercial bus operator or used bus dealer and either having a conversion firm do the interior or doing it yourself. There are some alternatives but most of them are relatively rare. Some converted coach owners have

---

Preceding Page: **For more than a decade, the Prevost LeMirage has been the most popular new coach shell for conversions and has outsold all of the other new coach shells combined. One major reason for its popularity is a long list of conversion options including door and window placement, extra height, larger engines and other special features. Originally introduced in 1977, the LeMirage is still currently available with a length of 40 feet and a width of 102 inches.** ROBERT REDDEN/REDDEN ARCHIVES.

been lucky enough to own or manage companies that have skilled professionals capable of doing a coach conversion. Home-made conversions in new shells are very rare but do exist. I have also seen coach interiors that were partially done by a professional conversion firm and partially by the coach owner. In addition, it is also possible to purchase a used converted coach that was converted by someone other than a professional conversion firm.

New coach shells and conversions are obviously the most expensive alternative but also may be the most rewarding. They give the converted coach owners the maximum possibilities in selecting the various options and amenities they desire. Typically, the prospective coach owner picks both a coach and a conversion firm and then sits down with people from the conversion firm to plan and design the coach interior and systems. It might be noted that some conversion firms have rather definite ideas about shells and systems and may wish to stay within the confines of what they know and trust. If you elect to go this route, the information in this book will help in selecting various options and in getting you started with operations. For the record it might be noted that in 1991, total prices on new coach conversions (both shell and conversion) range from about $400,000 to $650,000.

Purchasing a used converted coach done by a professional conversion firm has substantial merit if your budget is limited. It effectively gives you most of the advantages of a new coach professional conversion but at a lower price. On the positive side, most professional conversions were done in new coach shells so that the overall mileage of the unit may be relatively low. On the negative side, you have to take into consideration the wear and tear as well as the level of maintenance provided by the previous coach owner. Experience shows that a first coach is rarely also the last, so it is entirely within reason to purchase one that may not meet all of your initial criteria. As you become more familiar with converted coaches, your criteria will undoubtedly change and meanwhile, you are building up equity in a coach that could be used for a down payment on the next unit. Prices for used converted coaches with professional conversions vary considerably. There are some older and shorter used converted coaches on the market with prices as low as $25,000, while some of the newer used units sell in excess of $350,000. Somewhat obviously, there is a wide range of coaches with prices in between those extremes.

It is also possible to purchase a used converted coach that was converted by someone other than a professional conversion firm. Many have attractive interiors, but the shell mileage may be rather high, the systems work may be sadly lacking, and the resale value is questionable. My editor, Mike Gallagher, has his own horror story in this regard and now insists that no one recommends the purchase of such a unit except the individual selling it. It is extremely difficult to evaluate a situation like this, and the potential buyer is pretty much on his or her own.

The third option is to purchase a used shell, usually a commercial bus from a bus operator or dealer. This has a distinct advantage in price but may have the disadvantage of a substantial number of miles on the coach. In addition, you have to cope with any damage to the coach or the level of maintenance provided by the previous owner.

Most newcomers to coaches have some difficulty at first grasping the concepts of price versus condition, and operating condition versus desired or optimum condition. Novices tend to think that the cheapest bus is the best buy, which is usually incorrect, or that you need not put any work into a used coach, which is also incorrect. Most used buses on the market may be in good or at least passable operating condition but fall short of what I want. As a result, my experience has shown that with three of my last four coaches, after I purchase a coach I put another $10,000 to $15,000 into it to bring it up to my standards. Hence, it should be evident that a $30,000 coach that requires $5,000 in extra work is a better buy than a $25,000 coach that requires $15,000 in extra work. Prices on used coaches vary considerably. The really old ones sell for less than $10,000 while the newest units on the used market can go as high as $200,000.

If you elect to go with a used coach shell, you have two choices in regard to the interior. There are several professional conversion firms that work with used shells and will put in a very nice conversion for a reasonable price. As with new conversions, it is difficult to overrate the advantages of a professional conversion. They not only have the advantage of expertise in carpentry, electrical work and plumbing, but also the experience of having done similar jobs in the past. An interesting point is that professional coversions usually turn out to be much more workable because of better space utilization and better component design. Your only other choice is to do the conversion yourself.

Many people elect to do their own conversion work, and some have had excellent results. This is usually frowned upon by the professionals in the business. Most individuals lack the proper carpentry, plumbing and electrical skills to do a professional job although the finished interior may look more than presentable. The advantages of a professional conversion firm are more evident in design and purchasing as well as the selection and installation of the systems and components, much of which are not immediately evident but go a long way toward making the coach workable. The other disadvantages of doing the work yourself are safety and operations. It is extremely rare that an individual possesses the skills and experience offered by a conversion firm. Hence, people who attempt home made conversions run the risk of injuring themselves, their passengers or producing a coach that is less workable. As a result, most of the professionals are reluctant to encourage this.

Regardless of which of the above methods you select, there are a few places you can go for help. *National Bus Trader* magazine often has helpful articles on equipment and components as well as advertisements offering coaches and equipment. Many of the advertisers in *National Bus Trader* provide assistance to individuals who purchase buses or components. Write to 9698 West Judson Road, Polo, Illinois 61064, or phone (815) 946-2341 for a sample copy. A second source is the Family Motor Coach Association, 8291 Clough Pike, Cincinnati, Ohio 45244. Although this group includes RV's as well as coaches, membership is highly recommended. Their monthly magazine includes both helpful articles and helpful advertising. The best source for specific information is various clubs or organizations of converted coach owners. Many if not most will share information at rallies and meetings. There are several chapters of FMCA that fall within this category. The most active independent group is the Converted Coach Owners who may be contacted by writing to: Jan Sell, 903 North King Road, Toledo, Ohio 43617.

Past experience over the years with numerous novice converted coach owners has shown that many make one or more of three typical mistakes. Listing them here may help you in avoiding them.

1) Once having made the decision to own a converted coach, some people cannot resist the urge to go right out and purchase a used coach without any significant thought or planning on the matter. Once purchased, they come to me or others and ask what their second step should be. In unfortunately too many cases, they have already either purchased the wrong coach or have severely limited future options. Some years ago we had a support group here in the Midwest that you could call when you had an immediate urge to go out and buy a bus. They would send someone to come and sit with you until the insanity went away. And, yes, I was as guilty as the next guy in my younger years. However, with age and experience comes some common sense. Today, I strongly recommend that you do spend substantial time on planning and think your entire project through before going out to buy a coach.

2) The second typical mistake is mismatching the coach shell with the interior. You do not build a mansion in a slum, nor do you put an expensive diamond in a plastic setting. Likewise, there are some standards you should follow to stay within industry norms if you ever expect to sell the coach and get some money back out of it.

The basic question is how much of the total coach value should be represented by the shell and how much by the conversion? In virtually all cases, the ideal range is that the conversion should represent from 50% to 65% of the total coach value with the remainder being represented by the shell. A conversion by a professional conversion firm can get by with the conversion representing as much as two-thirds of total coach value. To insure resale potential, a nonprofessional conversion should stick closer to the 50/50 figure.

In virtually all cases, a higher percentage of shell value makes the coach easier to sell and once the shell drops below 30% of total value, the coach becomes difficult to sell. Hence, if you want to put a $60,000 interior into your coach, make sure that your shell is worth *at least* $30,000.

3) Many people select a shell for the wrong reasons. Purchasing a particular coach solely because it has a low price or something unusual will get you in trouble faster than anything else. However, it may be difficult for the novice with coaches to understand meaningful criteria and possibilities. The following information will hopefully help in that respect.

Care should be taken in regard to the value of conversions and the shell they will go into. Shown is a General Motors PD4104 which was built from 1953 to 1960 and at one time represented the most popular conversion shell on the highways. Today, the value of the shell is so low that it is inappropriate for most new conversions. ROBERT REDDEN/REDDEN ARCHIVES.

To begin with, there are four basic types of buses. From bottom to top, you have school buses, city-type transit buses, suburban-type buses and intercity coaches. Both school buses and transit-type buses have been converted to private coach use, and some of them have turned out to be very attractive. However, the professionals and experts will almost always opt for an intercity coach for a conversion and would rather have an older intercity coach shell rather than a newer school bus or transit bus shell. There are several reasons for this. The intercity coach is designed for sustained high speed travel on major highways. Many of the school buses and transit buses are simply not designed for this. The intercity coach has underfloor luggage compartments which offer a very handy location for conversion components and systems. The intercity coach is also the best built and hence the safest and most durable. It is not at all unusual for intercity coaches to turn two million miles, and there are converted private coaches on the highway celebrating their 50th birthday. Finally, intercity coaches are better insulated against loss of both heat and air conditioning. This will be very important to you the first time you spend a night in a coach in very cold or very hot weather.

For the record, suburban-type buses represent a mid-ground between the school and transit buses on the low end and intercity coaches on the high end. Most were built by General Motors from 1960 through the late 70s and carry a model number starting with SDM or SDH, although the Flxible Company built many comparable units. Constructed with a transit-type body, they were built for higher speed operation and many were equipped with a stick shift and some underfloor luggage space. As a result, they have some of the advantages of an intercity coach but some of the disadvantages of a transit bus.

Unfortunately, it is impossible to go beyond general information and criteria in a basic book like this. However, there are other sources of information available if you are interested. If you are looking for more detailed information on the manufacturers and models of intercity coaches, you can pick up a copy of a new book titled *Modern Intercity Coaches*. It was produced by the staff of *National Bus Trader* magazine and is slated for publication by

Transportation Trails in 1992. Although somewhat historical and quite large, it does provide a great deal of information on specific models including photographs and dimensions. We refrain from putting prices of used coaches in this book because they are quickly outdated. For this information you can refer to the "Round Up" pricing guide to used coaches which appears in alternate issues of *National Bus Trader*. Finally, for specific information on both new and used coaches, you can contact the dealers and conversion firms who regularly advertise in the pages of *National Bus Trader*.

New Coaches

New coach shells are the easiest to select but are also the most expensive. Current prices on only the shell can range up to the $200,000 level depending upon options. There are currently seven different intercity coach makes produced or sold in the United States and Canada. Three of these are imported from Europe and include Kassbohrer's Setra, two models offered by Van Hool and the LAG 350-T. To date, the number of conversions produced in these imports is very small and can be counted on the fingers of one hand. Hence, with due respect to the dealers involved, we will exclude them from this discussion for the sake of brevity. The remaining four makes represent established companies manufacturing in the United States and Canada. Brief details on these are as follows:

Motor Coach Industries — This company currently manufactures intercity coaches at plants in Winnipeg, Manitoba and Pembina, North Dakota. An affiliated company known as Transportation Manufacturing Corporation produced the same models at a plant in Roswell, New Mexico until recently when the intercity coach production was suspended but transit bus production continued at that location. MCI has long been affiliated with the Greyhound name and became a full subsidiary of the Greyhound Corp. in 1958. Most coaches purchased by Greyhound Lines since the late 1960s have been MCI's. The corporate relationships changed slightly in the late 1980s when Greyhound Corp. sold its subsidiary operating company, Greyhound Lines, to new owners but retained its bus manufacturing subsidiaries including MCI. Since then, Greyhound Corp. has changed its name to Dial Corp. and has continued to retain ownership of MCI through late 1991.

There are several advantages in selecting an MCI as a new conversion shell. They have been the most popular new coach on the U.S. and Canadian market for the past two decades. At

MCI's model 102C3 was first introduced in 1988 as a commercial coach and was made available as a conversion shell some months later. It has a length of 40 feet, a width of 102 inches, a fully paintable exterior, plus the tried-and-true MCI running gear. This example of the 102C3 was converted by Custom Coach Corp. with one of their semi-stock Landcruiser® interiors. © 1991 HIGH TIDES PHOTOGRAPHY/CUSTOM COACH CORP.

any time during this period they represented at least 60% of industry sales — more than all the other manufacturers put together. Hence, MCI has been selected by the greatest number of buyers and is found in the greatest number on the highways. This volume of numbers insures excellent parts availability and service since, in addition to the usual parts supply places, most commercial bus garages will have MCI parts. A second advantage is that MCI's traditionally have a high stainless steel content which makes them less prone to rust than many of the other coaches on the highway. It might also be mentioned that MCI does provide a conversion shell package with various options including a higher roof, larger engines and the elimination of some side windows. Currently, the most popular MCI conversion shell is their model 102C3 which was first introduced in 1988. This is 40 feet long, 102 inches wide, and has flat, paintable exterior sides plus a hint of European styling.

Several different Eagle models were manufactured from 1958 to 1990. Since 1988, lengths of 35, 40 and 45 feet were available with a width of 102 inches. Eagles have traditionally been a favorite of the entertainers as shown by this photo of an Eagle used by Tammy Wynette. ROBERT REDDEN/REDDEN ARCHIVES.

The MCI shell is most often selected by individuals who have a background in the commercial bus industry and those who have to be at places by a specific time and hence place a high value on repairability and parts availability. One of the most obvious advantages of an MCI is that in the event of an on-the-road problem, you can often go to a nearby bus garage for help.

Eagle Bus Manufacturing — Over the years, the Eagle name has been closely associated with Trailways operators. The original Eagle design was developed in Europe in the late 1950s and manufacturing was moved to Brownsville, Texas in 1974. The company manufacturing Eagles was at different times a subsidiary of Continental Trailways and more recently of Trailways, Inc. This situation changed in 1987 when Greyhound Lines (not Greyhound/Dial Corp.) acquired Trailways, Inc. and its subsidiaries. Hence, the Eagle and Greyhound names were connected for the first time. Due to the recent bankruptcy of Greyhound Lines, Eagle production at Brownsville was suspended in December of 1990. Current information suggests that the assembly line will start up again in 1992 under new ownership.

Eagles are different in that they offer a suspension based on the B.F. Goodrich torsilastic® rubber system rather than the air bags used on most other coaches on the market. Originally developed during World War II for military vehicles, this does provide different suspension characteristics than air ride and some people consider it superior. The other noteworthy characteristic of the Eagle is that it has retained a 12-volt electrical system while most other coaches have gone to a 24-volt system. Over the past two decades, the Eagle has been the second most popular coach on the U.S. and Canadian market and hence it can be said to have the numbers and parts availability second only to MCI. The Eagle has also developed quite a following as a conversion shell and was the most popular coach among Nashville entertainers for many years. Conversion shell packages are available with several options. I might also mention that many of the old-time convertors have a high regard for the Eagle as a conversion shell because it has a flat floor behind the driver and the sturdy steel-cage construction allows you to poke holes and hang things virtually anywhere.

The most popular Eagle shell in recent years has been their Model 15 which is 40 feet long and 102 inches wide. Since 1988, Eagle has also provided a companion 35-foot coach as well as a 45-foot coach. The 45-foot unit makes a delightful conversion shell but runs the risk of running afoul of highway length restrictions in several states. Eagles are most often selected by commercial coach operators, entertainers, those that want torsilastic® suspension, and many experienced bus and conversion people who simply have a high regard for an Eagle.

Prevost Car — The only company on the U.S. and Canadian scene that could be classed as an independent is Prevost Car which has two plants in Ste. Claire, Quebec, not far from Quebec City. Originally founded in 1919 by Eugene Prevost as a manufacturer of furniture, Prevost now produces intercity buses exclu-

Prevost's newest model, the H3-40, could be classed as the top-of-the-line conversion shell in 1991 in both features and price. It offers a length of 40 feet, a width of 102 inches, plus numerous technological advances. This one was converted by American Coach in Michigan and carried a price tag of approximately $650,000 in mid-1991. DAVID PLACHNO.

sively. In recent years, Prevost has developed quite a reputation for technological advancement. In 1967 they were the first manufacturer to build 40-foot long coaches for the general inter-city bus industry. Their LeMirage, introduced in 1977 with large passenger windows, was the first domestically produced coach to offer a hint of European styling. In 1984, they became the first manufacturer to switch exclusively to the new 102-inch width. A year later, in 1985, they introduced their 60-foot long H5-60, the first production articulated intercity coach in the United States and Canada. Their new "H" series offers several technological advancements and has been augmented by the new H3-40 model which is 40 feet long and 102 inches wide. The H3-40 also offers substantial stainless steel in its construction.

For at least the last decade, Prevost has led the new coach shell market in sales and represents more than 60% of all new coaches sold for conversions. There are at least two reasons for this. One is that since 1979, their 40-foot coaches have been available off the production line as shell packages with an amaz-ing number of options including engines, door placement, win-dow placement, roof height, systems and components. The shells are ordered direct from the factory on a form that provides prices and options. A second reason is that Prevost has endeared itself to many of the major conversion firms with numerous options as well as a floor planning program. As of 1991, the Prevost LeMirage continues as the most popular new conversion shell on the market. However, their more expensive but technologically advanced H3-40 has taken the attention of higher-priced conver-sion owners and is starting to sell in increasingly greater numbers.

Prevost shells traditionally appeal to those people coming from RV ownership who place a high regard on options and want a coach that has more RV features in what is still a commercial intercity bus shell. However, new Prevosts have also become popular with some of the old-timers in the business including many of the entertainers. As of this writing, Prevost has not yet offered a conversion shell option on their 60-foot H5-60 articulated coach. When and if that happens, the H5-60 will quickly become the epitome of conversion shells.

Neoplan U.S.A. Corporation — A European bus builder based in Stuttgart, West Germany, Neoplan began importing intercity coaches to the U.S. and Canada in the 1970s and reached a substantial import volume in the early 1980s. Neoplan U.S.A. Corporation was founded to build a bus factory in Lamar, Colorado that opened in 1981 to produce transit buses. Production of the intercity models was started in Colorado in the later 1980s.

Neoplan currently offers five different intercity models including the less-expensive Metroliner, two bread-and-butter charter/tour coaches (Jetliner and Cityliner), the high-deck and very elegant Spaceliner, and the unusual double-deck Skyliner. Incidentally, the Skyliner is the only production double-deck coach currently made in the U.S. and Canada. Neoplan shells offer two noteworthy advantages. One is that they provide unusual European styling with smooth sides and attractive

Although built in Lamar, Colorado primarily from domestic componentry, Neoplans have a rather exotic European appearance. Completed in 1991, this special order Spaceliner shell had a length of 45 feet, special openable windows, and a 500-horsepower Detroit Diesel engine. With the exception of their Skyliner double-decker, virtually all of the Neoplan intercity coaches have served as conversion shells. NEOPLAN U.S.A.

design. Particularly noteworthy in this regard is the Spaceliner which offers a high windshield and passenger level that permits putting a living area at the front above the driver's compartment. Neoplan's second advantage is that they can offer a wide range of options. For example, they recently produced a 45-foot Spaceliner shell with openable windows on a special order for a customer.

Typical Neoplan owners are people who want a coach with unusual styling or design appeal or those who want an option not available from the other manufacturers. Although Neoplan shells have not been produced and sold in large numbers in the past, their popularity is currently on the increase.

Used Coach Shells

Earlier coaches originally produced by the above four new coach manufacturers are currently available on the used coach market. In addition, there are two other manufacturers, both no longer producing intercity coaches, that are popular as used coach conversion shells.

Flxible Company — Originally founded in 1913 in Loudonville, Ohio to manufacture motorcycle side cars, the Flxible Company produced intercity coaches as late as 1970. Following more recent corporate changes, the company today is headquartered in Delaware, Ohio and is a major transit bus builder. Noteworthy models through the years include Flxible's little round-back Clipper, known later under several names including Visicoach and Starliner, which originally founded the commercial converted coach industry in the late 1940s.

Perhaps more noteworthy from a current standpoint are three 35-foot long Flxible models produced between 1955 and 1970 known as the VL-100, Hi-Level and Flxliner. They offered an interesting combination of torsilastic® suspension, Flxible's traditional economical operation, and a simple design that was easy to repair. They were also among the few U.S.-built coaches to offer a synchromesh manual transmission. Since they were only produced in small numbers, it would be rare to find one today still in commercial service. However, many of them were converted and can still be seen today on the highways. Those people who own them seem to like them but their age is starting to show from the standpoint of service and replacement parts. However, due in large part to continued production of similar units in Mexico and a dealer in Michigan, many of the most important parts are still readily available.

General Motors Corporation — The General Motors Bus and Coach Division can trace its history back to 1917 when John D. Hertz began building taxicabs in Chicago. For at least three decades, GM was the largest and most prominent builder of both intercity and transit buses in the United States. In fact, the bus industry's extensive use of Detroit Diesel engines stems from this period. General Motors discontinued intercity coach production in 1980 and sold its transit bus production to the bus manufacturing segment of Greyhound/Dial Corp. later in the decade.

Very popular as conversion shells were three 35-foot Flxible models built between 1955 and 1970 known as the VL-100, Hi-Level and Flxliner. Shown is a Flxliner which was professionally converted by Angola Coach in Indiana. Many of these coaches have been converted and are still in operation. LARRY PLACHNO.

GM Coaches differ from most of the other coaches on the market in that they embraced the V-drive transmission in the late 1930s and stayed with it until the end of production. The two major advantages of this are that the V-drive generally provides more interior coach space and is usually easier to work on. The negative features are that the coaches are limited to V-drive components and that intercity automatic transmissions never became really popular in V-drive coaches.

At least two GM models have been very prominent as a conversion shell. The 35-foot PD4104, built 1953-1960, was a revolutionary coach and dominated the conversion industry for at least a decade. It was followed by the PD4106 (built 1961-1965), which was less popular but had a good following. Both coaches had the advantage of being extremely well built and relatively economical (the PD4106 occasionally was reported in at 10 miles per gallon) but have declined in popularity because of their age and parts availability.

Other GM coaches have been used for conversion shells but have been less popular. Noteworthy are the PD4501 *Scenicruisers* built by General Motors for Greyhound from 1954 to 1956 but eventually sold on the used market. In contrast to most GM coaches, they were equipped with a conventional drive train rather than the typical V-drive arrangement. Considered by many to be the finest intercity coach ever built, the *Scenicruiser* was converted in respectable numbers but has a reputation for being a difficult conversion shell because of its two levels and seat platforms. GM coaches built between 1966 and 1980, both 35-foot and 40-foot models, are known as "Buffalo Buses" because of the step and hump at the front. They are generally reliable and many have been successfully converted. However, they are less popular as conversion shells because of the front steps and increasing problems with parts availability.

There are several reasonable criteria that can be used in the selection of a used coach. Following are the ones that are frequently brought up. Obviously, your own decision is based on which of the criteria you wish to emphasize.

Repairability and Parts — If you use your coach for serious travel, repairability and parts availability may be a major criteria. Age is a major factor since older coaches tend to have more problems in parts availability and in finding knowledgeable service people. Beyond that, coaches in more widespread use, such as the MCI and Eagle, have an advantage in this area.

Longevity and Durability — Most intercity coaches will survive many miles and many years with proper care. However, a major factor in this area is the prevention of rust. Both the MCI's as well as the new Prevost H3-40 have an advantage with their stainless steel construction. GM coaches had high aluminum content and Eagles have had aluminum sides. Eagles built since late 1988 have substantial Cor-Ten steel in their construction.

Suspension Systems — Some people consider coach suspension to be a major criteria. Both the Eagles and the larger Flxibles have torsilastic® suspension. The other coaches have air ride although Neoplan does offer an unusual independent suspension system.

Exterior Design — Neoplan has the advantage in unique styling and exterior design. However, the Prevost coaches are very appealing and MCI's new smooth-sided 102C3 has some good possibilities.

Interior Configuration — Coaches with flat floors are generally considered the easiest to convert. Those without flat floors include the GM coaches produced after 1966, the *Scenicruiser*, and early MC-7's with seat platforms. The MC-6, with its three passenger levels plus bells and whistles, has been nicely converted but is no coach for a novice. In addition, many Eagles have a step at the front but this is generally not seen as a major conversion problem. An interesting side note is that some coaches have flat floors that are not level but slope slightly upward toward the rear. This is not necessarily a problem during conversion if the people involved are aware of it.

Conversion Options and Features — If you are planning to purchase a used coach that has been operated commercially, it is unlikely to have any special conversion options. However, this may be an important criteria in regard to new coaches. Prevost easily has more available conversion options, both MCI and Eagle offer some, and Neoplan is willing to consider customer requests.

Coach Length — You really have only two basic choices. Most of the older coaches are 35 feet long while most of the newer ones are 40 feet long. There are exceptions since both older Eagles and *Scenicruisers* are 40 feet long and both Eagle and Neoplan have produced 35-foot coaches in recent years. Concerns about the 40-foot coaches in regard to campgrounds and back roads are generally overrated and many people have made the upward transition without significant problems. Eagle had offered a 45-foot coach, which has some marvelous interior possibilities, but exceeds highway length restrictions in many states.

Transmissions — Automatic transmissions did not become popular until the early 1970s. With very few exceptions, coaches built before this period and many built in more recent times are equipped with manual transmissions. It is technically possible to replace a manual transmission with an automatic but this is rarely

This 1974 General Motors P8M4905A was professionally converted by Southern Comfort Coach in 1988. Built between 1966 and 1980, these GM "Buffalo Buses" have excellent operational characteristics but are less popular as conversion shells because of the steps next to the driver and increasing problems with parts availability. LARRY PLACHNO.

cost-effective with an older coach. Most of the individuals look-ing for a used coach with an automatic transmission end up with a 40-foot MCI from the MC-7 onward although you can find automatics in some of the other makes and models.

Selecting a used coach is a relatively complex procedure but there are some general criteria that apply. Coaches with less overall mileage are considered better than those with more overall mileage if they were subject to the same level of maintenance. However, the numbers bear no relation to your experience with automobiles. A used commercial coach with 500,000 total miles is still considered relatively new and any number significantly less than that might be considered particularly interesting depend-ing on circumstances.

Likewise, engine mileage is an important factor. Depending on usage and maintenance, a Detroit Diesel coach engine can go 300,000 to 500,000 miles between major overhauls, and an overhaul is a major expense item. Hence, engines with low mileage are particularly advantageous when purchasing a coach for conversion.

Some attention should be given to body condition. Dings and dents may not detract from operational ability but they are ex-pensive to replace and repair. Internal systems are difficult to evaluate unless you have enough knowledge to know which items are important and which are easily repaired or replaced. However, any novice can look for serious rust problems, particularly on frame members and engine bulkheads and especially on coaches with conventional steel instead of stainless steel or aluminum. Virtually every coach has a little rust and in the right places it may not be significant. However, major structural damage from rust is expensive to repair and may be a good indication that you should look at another bus.

You should also look for evidence of any collisions. Major col-lision damage, even if seemingly repaired, often makes a coach less suitable for continued operation. There may be hidden damage that has not or cannot be repaired, or maybe there are bent frame members that will cause problems for the coach owner.

If you do purchase a used coach, my suggestion is that your first stop should be a competent bus garage so that any problems can be repaired immediately. At the same time you can have work done on the coach to bring it up to your specifications. As mentioned earlier, it is very rare to purchase a used coach and not have some work facing you when you get home.

Beyond the obvious fuel and oil checks, the first thing I do when taking ownership of a used bus is to immediately replace the fuel filters. Clogged fuel filters are one of the major reasons for buses quitting while on the road. Next, I inspect and replace the belts and hoses, which are also inexpensive items that can lead to coach failure. After this, I set up a preventive maintenance program for the coach which is covered in Chapter 5.   ⚊

Still popular on the used market for shorter conversion shells are the several 35-foot MCI's built from 1964 to 1980. They have relatively flat floors and enjoy substantial parts availability. This MC-5C was professionally converted from a used commercial coach and was photographed in Arizona. TED ROTH/NATIONAL BUS TRADER COLLECTION.

Popular Intercity Coach Shells

Following is a brief list of the more popular intercity coach shells used for coach conversions in recent years. Additional details can be found in the book titled *Modern Intercity Coaches* available from Transportation Trails in 1992.

Model	Years Built	Length in feet	Width in inches	Underfloor Capacity in cu. ft.	Axles
EAGLE					
Model 01	1960-1968	40	96	330?	3
Model 05	1968-1980	40	96	330	3
Model 07	1969	40	102	350	3
Model 10	1980-1989	40	96	316	3
Model 15/35	1988-1990	35	102	225	2
Model 15/40	1985-1990	40	102	345	3
Model 15/45	1988-1990	45	102	450	3
FLXIBLE					
Clipper etc.	1937-1967	35[1]	95½	—	2
VL-100	1955-1959	35	95½	184[2]	2
Hi-Level	1960-1962	35	95½	184	2
Flxliner	1964-1970	35	95½	184	2
GMC (General Motors Corporation)					
PD4104	1953-1960	35	95½	212	2
PD4501 Scenicruiser	1954-1956	40	96	344	3
PD4106	1961-1965	35	95½	205	2
PD4107/P8M4108A	1966-1978	35	96	290	2
PD4903-05/H8H-649	1968-1980	40	96	290[3]	3[4]
MCI (Motor Coach Industries)					
MC-5A/MC-5B	1964-1977	35	96	212	2
MC-5C	1977-1980	35	96	202	2
MC-6	1969-1970	40	102	450	3
MC-7	1968-1973	40	96	325	3
MC-8	1973-1978	40	96	300	3
MC-9	1978-1990	40	96	300	3
102A3	1978-1990	40	102	319	3
102C3	1988 on	40	102	319	3
NEOPLAN USA					
Metroliner AN340/3	1984 on	40	102	400[5]	3[4]
Jetliner AN240/3	1987 on	40[6]	102	340	3
Cityliner AN116/3	1986 on[7]	40[6]	102	360	3
Spaceliner AN117/3	1988 on[7]	40	102	460	3

Continued on next page

Popular Intercity Coach Shells
(continued)

Model	Years Built	Length in feet	Width in inches	Underfloor Capacity in cu. ft.	Axles
		PREVOST CAR			
Champion	1967-1982	35/40	96	?	2/3
Prestige	1968-1981	35/40	96	?	2/3
LeMirage	1976-1983	35/40	96	?	2/3
LeMirage XL	1984 on	40	102	?	3
H3-40	1989 on	40	102	420	3

NOTES

1 - Many of the earlier coaches were shorter.

2 - VL-100's built 1955-1957 have slightly less capacity.

3 - 290 cubic feet standard on 3-axle 40-foot Buffalo Buses. 2-axle 40-footers had 403 cubic feet.

4 - Several built with only two axles.

5 - On two-axle coaches. Less on three-axle coaches.

6 - Also produced in smaller lengths with correspondingly less underfloor luggage capacity.

7 - Earlier coaches of this model, built in Europe, were imported and converted.

2

Conversion Interior Design and Styling

While the first chapter of this book covered primarily the outside or shell of the coach, this chapter will primarily deal with the interior of the converted coach. The following chapter will, in turn, be dedicated to converted coach systems. Regardless of whether you have a conversion firm do the interior for you, or you purchase a used conversion, you should know the various options available.

Traditionally, each converted coach is unique in that its arrangement of interior and systems reflects the needs and wishes of the coach owner. Recently, there have also been some converted coach interiors built on a factory system with standard interiors designed to please a wide range of potential new owners. Although the standard interiors are deplored by many traditional coach owners as the influence of factory RV's in coaches, they are admittedly difficult to tell from true custom-built interiors. In any event, when dealing with converted coaches it is well to remember that they are unique or at least are expected to be unique. Admittedly, there are limits from the standpoint of component parts and the practicality of some ideas, but beyond that you are on your own. I have already seen converted coaches with a piano, organ, fireplace, a Jacuzzi almost large enough for swimming, a rooftop patio, a trailer with a boat and automobile, an

Preceding Page: **The more expensive converted coaches have been moving away from conventional RV interiors and many no longer even look like buses on the inside. Shown is the interior of a 1978 MC-8 which was converted by JM Coachworks for an entertainer and his family. Note the semi-formal dining area instead of a dinette, the L-shaped kitchen, and lack of an obvious bus appearance.** JM COACHWORKS.

exercise ramp hidden under a couch, and a full-fledged computerized office hidden under a queen bed. The possibilities are virtually limitless.

Types of Conversions

Technically, there are several types of conversions. I have found it convenient to classify them in four different major categories, primarily by usage, which tends to cover virtually all possibilities. Although you may not be interested in more than one of these types, it would be helpful to know that they exist and how they differ.

The *motorhome* conversion provides an interior similar to an RV so that two or more people can travel and live in the coach. Typically, it contains beds, a galley or kitchen, a bathroom and

Party coaches are generally owned by commercial charter bus operators and represent the simplest interior modifications. They normally retain most of the conventional bus seating but have some additional features and amenities. This MC-5A party coach was owned by the author in the early 1980s and contained four tables plus a non-electric galley. CHUCK BOIE/NATIONAL BUS TRADER COLLECTION.

some type of living area. Both the quality and type of interior may vary substantially from a simple arrangement with several beds for weekend family trips to a sophisticated interior for a retired couple who actually use their coach for a permanent residence (and are called "full timers"). Most have relatively sophisticated systems including an auxiliary generator and most can be hooked into campground's electric, water and sewer systems. Virtually all coaches of this type are owned and driven by the people who use them.

As the name indicates, *entertainer coaches* are used by entertainers to get from one performance to the next. Coaches work very well for this type of service since the entertainers usually have staff and equipment, and sometimes even their family members, to move with them. Using public transportation for this purpose would be difficult. However, with a converted coach, entertainers can be on their way and be either comfortable or asleep within an hour after a performance.

Entertainer coaches usually come in two different types. The lead entertainer and family usually use a converted coach with an interior very similar to a motorhome, although usually a little more fancy and expensive. If there is a supporting crew or cast, they use what is usually known as either a "bunk bus" or "crew coach." This consists of individual bunks on each side of the aisle for each member of the crew, often with individual lighting and entertainment systems. The bunk bus or crew coach usually has a small living area for daytime travel as well as a small galley. In most cases the entertainers do not drive their own coaches but hire individuals who handle the driving and oversee the coach. Some of these coaches are owned by the entertainers while others are converted and leased by companies that specialize in this type of unit.

Both *party coaches* and *executive coaches* belong to the commercial side of the business. They are owned and operated by commercial bus companies and are chartered to groups on an hourly or mileage basis. Party coaches generally retain standard bus seating but passenger capacity may be reduced slightly because of the addition of other features such as tables and a simple galley.

Most party coaches will not have elaborate underfloor conversion systems, they often retain a commercial rather than an RV bathroom, and they rarely have a generator and the proper equipment for hooking up at campgrounds. Party coaches are almost never equipped with beds or overnight equipment.

Executive coaches differ in that they have a fully converted interior. Instead of bus seats, they will have couches, individual chairs, and tables. Sophisticated entertainment including a good audio system and TV video system is expected. Most contain a rather elaborate galley, an RV-type toilet and at least some underfloor systems possibly including water and an auxiliary generator. Overall capacity tends to be limited, in the range of 18 to 30 seated passengers in a 40-foot coach. Some executive coaches are built with couches that convert to beds, a shower, a generator, and campground hook ups so that they can be used for overnight sleeping for a limited number. Some are so

Executive coaches have a fully converted interior but are designed for luxury transportation rather than camping. Interiors usually include couches, individual chairs, tables and some type of galley. This example was converted by Custom Coach in 1989 using a new MCI shell. LARRY PLACHNO.

sophisticated that they contain underfloor systems fully equal to a motorhome-type unit.

The fourth group can best be described as the *commercial* or *business* category. They serve a wide range of applications relating to various business purposes. Most are owned by the companies that use them.

Some are equipped as mobile offices. In this case the interior and systems may be very similar to a motorhome with the addition of office equipment, possibly including desks, typewriters, file equipment, telephones, and even a copier and fax machine. Many are set up as mobile showrooms for various products and services and may include a small living and sleeping area for the driving and sales people who stay with the coach. Others I have seen can be rather unusual and exotic. For example, a major beer brewer once had several coaches equipped with bars and seats

Among the more unusual business conversions seen in recent years was this MCI operated by the Budweiser people. Although looking somewhat like an executive coach, the fully-equipped bar at the rear was used for training bartenders in the proper method of dispensing the owner's beverage. Beer could also be dispensed from a spout on the side of the coach and special compartments were provided underneath the coach for the beer kegs. LARRY PLACHNO.

to teach bartenders the proper method of pouring and dispensing their beverage. I also saw a coach set up with an elaborate audio visual theater in the rear for selling the company's products and services. The front portion of the coach contained a small living area and beds for a crew of two.

Admittedly, there are several converted coaches that really do not fall into one of the above categories. A good example are the bloodmobiles and similar units designed for some type of medical testing. There are also special coaches designed specifically for the transportation of individuals who require specialized attention and medical equipment.

Since the majority of individuals who contact us are interested in the more conventional type of motorhome interiors, we will concentrate on that in this chapter. However, much of this information on interiors and systems may still pertain to the other types of conversions.

Motorhome Conversion Interiors

Most motorhome interiors represent total conversions. If you are starting with a used coach, the entire interior is removed with the possible exception of the driver's area and dash. New coaches built specifically as motorhome shells are usually delivered with a totally empty interior looking not unlike an empty boxcar although it may have some plywood paneling on the walls.

During the conversion process, the floor, walls and ceiling are then covered with new materials. It might be noted that converted coaches should be fitted with as much insulation as possible since metal construction plus the large window area creates particular problems in preserving heat or air conditioning. A sure sign of a nonprofessional conversion is paneling or other wall coverings affixed directly to the coach walls without benefit of intermediate insulation, and even some of the professional conversions could use more insulation. To quote Mike Gallagher, ''. . . you can't have too much.''

Traditionally, the walls, structures, tables, cabinetry, and possibly some of the furniture are made from wood. Plywood is typically used for a base with the surface determined by the new coach owner. In past years, Formica was a popular finish for tables and other surfaces since it not only survived extremes of temperature but also could be easily cleaned. Some of the more expensive coaches have now gone to Corian or marble surfaces, and less expensive laminated surfaces of various types are seen in other coaches.

While beds, dinettes and couches are frequently hand made to suit a particular coach or owner, conventional chairs and couches can also be used. There are companies that specialize in making furniture for converted coaches, but standard furniture as found in a conventional furniture store is not unknown.

Most floors are carpeted although shag carpeting is generally avoided. Tile has been used for both kitchen and bathroom floors although some coach owners still prefer carpeting in these areas. Many coach owners, particularly those with children or who find tracked-in dirt to be a problem, use a runner to protect the carpet.

Wall coverings are pretty much left up to the discretion of the new coach owner. Carpeting has been used and although it has excellent insulation value, it may be difficult to keep clean and may not look good unless done by a professional. Formica and other laminates are very popular for walls since they are easy to clean. More expensive coaches get into more exotic walls and materials. Both wallpaper and custom wall treatments are not unknown and I have seen coaches with surfaces made of various types of animal hide including rattlesnake.

Headliners and ceiling materials are usually relatively simple in design. They are usually kept light in color since dark ceiling colors tend to make passengers feel uncomfortable. Some of the newer coaches are now putting extra equipment and items on the ceiling. This can include skylights as well as (if your ceiling height permits) some ductwork for ventilation.

In any event, your selection of interior materials should be compatible with your planned use of the coach. Some coach interiors are very exotic and beautiful but can only survive careful treatment by a retired couple. If you plan to travel with children or friends, or if you expect to have mud from campgrounds and sand from beaches tracked into your coach, you would be well advised to plan your interior accordingly.

The majority of motorhome conversions follow along rather conventional lines and offer only a limited number of options. Following are some of the more conventional arrangements.

Most converted coaches retain the standard passenger entry door at the right front and modify it only with the addition of a new covering and a keyed lock. There are converted coaches that have closed off the traditional front door and have installed a new door in the center of the coach. The only obvious merits in this are that your entry would be into the kitchen or galley area of the coach, which would avoid tracking mud into the living area, and the possibility of a more elaborate buddy seat ar-

Royal Coach in Indiana put this interior into a new Prevost LeMirage shell. Behind the lengthy couch is a semi-formal dinette opposite the galley area. Note that the aisle swings off to one side to provide a side aisle arrangement. DON BRAYTON/ROYAL COACH.

rangement. Coming from the commercial end of the business, I prefer the traditional right front door which is also the most economical arrangement.

Many if not most converted coach owners want some type of "copilot" or "buddy" seat at the right front so that a spouse, child or friend can sit in front to converse with the driver. This is usually matched with a trap door that can be lowered over the stepwell when the front door is closed. This can be simply a manual operation although the better converted coaches provide a trap door operated by an electric switch over an air cylinder. I have such a seat in my own coach and mine is equipped with a seat belt. Because of proximity to the front of the coach, our coach rules require passengers in that seat to have their seat belt on at all times.

Although the above is the standard arrangement, I have seen several alternatives. In most cases, the buddy seat can be wide enough for two people without blocking the aisle. In a few cases, I have seen the buddy seat moved over to the center of the coach adjacent to the driver's seat. This usually requires modifying your stepwell to a circular style which is not only expensive but also limits your interior possibilities. On at least one occasion I have seen a lounge chair used in place of a buddy seat. When fully reclined, the passenger's heels were nearly touching the windshield. I personally have an aversion to something like this for obvious safety reasons.

The driver's area on the coach is usually modified and added to rather than replaced. On coaches that require dash space for additional items (a TV screen for a back-up camera or an audio entertainment system are typical), the dash can be extended around the right side of the driver's seat in a semi-U style. I might suggest that whatever else you do, make sure that the driver is provided with an area to hold a cup of coffee, toll change and other receipts. My own current coach has a small folding table to the right of the driver, complete with cup holders, that is marvelous for this purpose.

(continued on page 48)

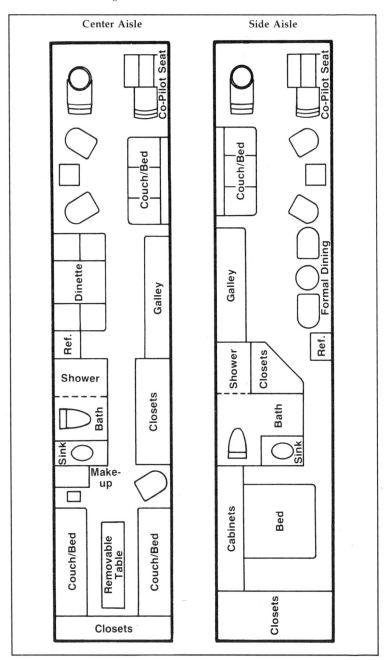

Traditional Interior Configurations

Experience over the years has shown that there are only a very few interior configurations that make the best use of space and work well for most people. The diagrams on the preceding page show two of the most popular arrangements.

On the left is the standard center aisle configuration. This provides a relatively narrow bathroom area but compensates with substantial closet space across the aisle. Twin beds are shown in the rear that can double as couches during the day, thus turning the rear bedroom into a daytime lounge area. If additional sleeping space is necessary, bunks can be placed over the beds, dinette, or front couch. Note that this arrangement usually has enough room left over for an extra chair or two in the rear bedroom area. This is a good configuration for coach owners who usually carry children or guests with them.

On the right is a side aisle configuration. This provides a larger bathroom area but you lose the closet space opposite the bathroom. Most people compensate for this by placing more closet space in the rear bedroom. A single larger bed is shown in the rear bedroom. In the diagram the headboard is placed sideways but it could also be placed to the front or rear of the coach. A twin bed arrangement is also possible. The drawing also shows a formal dining area in place of a dinette. This would be an appropriate configuration for a couple traveling alone or with an occasional guest. If the formal dining area were replaced with a traditional dinette, this arrangment could also be used for sleeping guests or children at the front of the coach.

Not shown is the newer walk-through bath arrangement where the bathroom extends entirely across the coach. This would be similar to the configuration on the left except that the aisle is actually incorporated into the bathroom. The walk-through bath substantially limits access to the rear of the coach while the bathroom is in use and is generally limited to coaches where a couple travels alone.

Many converted coach owners have someone replace the conventional driver's seat with something more comfortable, usually including air suspension and arm rests. The seat in my own coach has both a simple air suspension system as well as arm rests, and I recommend both for long-distance driving.

Traditionally, the area above the driver's head on the left is reserved for the master electrical controls for the coach. This has a great deal of merit since the driver can easily get at them while remaining in the driver's seat; it also prevents the passengers from messing with them. If you plan to travel with children or guests, you should seriously consider keeping this tradition. However, many newer coaches built for travel by only a couple have gone to either a master electrical panel in other areas or multiple controls throughout the coach. There admittedly is some merit in being able to reach out in your bed on a cold night to turn on your generator or heating system.

There are some conventional ways to insure privacy at the front of the coach when you are parked at night. A leather or canvas covering can be snapped in place either inside or outside the windshield, although most people prefer the inside version because of convenience. I have seen drapes used but they can create problems for the driver's field of vision if they do not extend back into the coach. Some coaches also have some type of cloth that can be hung immediately behind the driver. This may be of value if you intend to do extensive night driving and want to keep lights on in the remainder of the coach, but a windshield device is usually preferred for privacy.

Although converted coaches are expected to be unique, the areas behind the driver's seat are remarkably similar and offer only limited variation. Years of actual use on the road have dictated some conventions that work best, and very few converted coaches deviate from these plans to any extent. The convention calls for four different areas in order: living area, kitchen/galley, bathroom and possibly closets, and a rear bedroom.

Virtually all living areas on coaches have a center aisle with furniture on both sides of the aisle. The most popular arrangement is undoubtedly two chairs on one side of the aisle with a table in between, and a couch on the other side of the aisle. I happen to like swivel chairs so that they can either face forward, across the aisle to the couch, or turn to the table. Some variation is possible with the table. It can be a very simple table that either folds down or into the wall to provide extra space. It can also be permanent and extend down to the floor to house entertainment equipment or provide additional storage. I have also seen this table used for special purposes, such as housing a computer or typewriter. Some people have a TV installed above the driver's head facing toward the rear. The couch usually makes into a bed at night if you have a guest. If you need additional sleeping facilities, you can consider the merits of a bunk above the couch.

There are obviously many variations on this theme. I know a family with several children that had couches installed on both sides of the aisle with bunks above both. I also know a couple who did not want extra sleeping space and had chairs placed on both sides of the aisle. Some of the less expensive conversions also put conventional forward-facing bus seats in this area or individual forward-facing seats. This almost always detracts from the motorhome appearance but can be a viable alternative if you plan to carry several people.

As long as we are on the subject of furniture, I should mention the concept of cup holders. These are simply little circular metal holders in the tables and adjacent to the furniture to keep cups from spilling. Unfortunately, when not in use for cups and glasses, they have a tendency to be drafted for other sundry purposes. My children use them to hold spare change and toys while I have a bad habit of using them for spare parts and receipts. Some of the fancier coaches do not have them at all and other coach owners have mixed reactions. I tend to prefer them since they do tend to keep liquids from walking around and spilling on the carpet when you are driving.

Ash trays fall into this same category. However, many coach owners prohibit smoking on their coaches. If invited on board someone's coach, you would be well advised to ask first before lighting up or simply give up your tobacco habit for the duration.

Window treatment and lighting varies extensively from coach to coach. The easiest method of dealing with windows are simple drapes. More expensive coaches go into various types of blinds or shades, usually with extra woodwork to separate the windows. Lighting is up to the coach owner but I prefer a dual system. All four main areas of my own coach have both a.c. indirect fluorescent lighting as well as direct d.c. lighting. This not only gives me a choice of what electrical system I prefer to use but also gives me a choice in light intensity for different purposes. Fluorescent

Completed in 1991, this Custom Coach Landcruiser® interior in a new MCI 102C3 maintains many of the traditional conventions. In the front lounge area is a couch opposite two chairs separated by a table. Opposite the galley you might note the formal dining area instead of the traditional dinette. © 1991 HIGH TIDES PHOTOGRAPHY/CUSTOM COACH CORP.

lighting that operates from d.c. power is also available, which may be desirable in a coach planned for extensive remote camping where a.c. power may not be readily available. I have seen several coaches that have been converted with attractive decorator-type lighting that is often inadequate for reading maps and magazines.

Because of the similarity with yacht interiors, the cooking area on a coach is frequently called a galley. If more elaborate, it then becomes a kitchen. Basic galley equipment usually includes a countertop and sink (usually double), a microwave and a two-burner cook-top. Unless you are a gourmet chef, this tends to meet most needs. Obvious additions include a convection oven, additional cook-top burners and various built-in appliances including an ice maker, an ice chest, trash compactor, a toaster and a coffee maker.

If you are planning on living full time in your coach, I would suggest that you look at a more elaborate kitchen because you will probably be happier in the long run. If you plan on being in the coach for no more than two weeks at a time, you probably can survive with only the basics. Most coach owners eat out more often or prepare simpler meals than they originally expected. My own coach has only a microwave and a cook-top with two burners and in spite of the fact that I have cooked simple meals for up to four people, I have never needed more. I will admit that I do keep a toaster under the counter and bring it out and plug it in when I need it.

Most converted coaches are equipped with either a full-size or almost full-size refrigerator. If your coach is set up with the right systems, you can keep your refrigerator continually operating during your travels. Most converted coach refrigerators are powered either two or three ways. The two-way refrigerators can take d.c. power from a battery or a.c. power from a campground land line, an on-board inverter or your auxiliary generator. The three-way refrigerator will do the same but has the additional option of propane.

Galley areas are usually provided with a variety of storage areas both overhead and under the counter for cups, plates, napkins and eating utensils, as well as the expected canned and dry food. I might suggest that unless you plan on living in your coach on a full-time basis, a large pantry is usually not necessary. We find that two conventional drawers and a pair of overhead cabinets are more than sufficient for the cans and dry food needed for several people. Particularly since we often buy additional food and supplies along the way when we find something that we did not bring along.

I should mention that some arrangement should be made for trash since it is an inevitable problem in a converted coach. My current coach has a simple solution to this problem that I recommend if you are not planning anything more elaborate. The bottom of one of my galley cabinets has a short chute leading to a large kitchen trash container that is strapped in place in the underfloor luggage compartment with a bungee cord. This not

This European-type kitchen was installed on a Prevost LeMirage by Royal Coach in Indiana. Note the clean lines, uncluttered appearance and the matching cabinetry closer to the front of the coach. Opposite the galley is a matching dinette. DON BRAYTON/ROYAL COACH.

only gets the trash, but also any related odors, out of the living area and into the bottom of the coach. Disposing of the garbage is a simple matter of pulling the trash out of the underfloor compartment and putting a fresh plastic liner into the trash container.

Most coaches have some type of eating area either across the aisle or in close proximity to the galley. In years past, this was traditionally a dinette. When equipped with cup holders, a dinette can sit and feed as many as four people at a time with minimal mess. At night it can convert into a double bed, a real plus for those with large families. Some of the newer coaches built for only a couple have dispensed with the dinette because it does not fit with the decor and the extra sleeping area is not necessary. In its place is a small formal dining table and chairs; usually for two people but I have seen them large enough for four. If you do want a more formal dining area, I would suggest that you keep yourself from getting carried away with it. One couple I know

The prosaic dinette has been a tradition on converted coaches for four decades. Normally located adjacent to the galley, it serves the dual purpose of providing a convenient place to eat meals and also converts to a bed at night. This example is located in the author's coach. LARRY PLACHNO.

went to the trouble of having their conversion firm hang a beautiful chandelier above their dining table. It really added to the appearance of the coach but had the unfortunate habit of swinging against the side of the coach in a sharp turn.

Some of the newer conversions use angled lines in their bathrooms to both provide more space and eliminate the old fashioned square look. This bathroom was built by Custom Coach into a Prevost LeMirage shell. Note the angles on the sink, shower and mirrored medicine cabinet. © HIGH TIDES PHOTOGRAPHY/CUSTOM COACH CORP.

Your bathroom is easily the one area most subject to individual taste or need on your coach. Although there are minor variations, there are three basic configurations to select from.

The old, traditional design has a center aisle from your galley to your rear bedroom. The bathroom is located on one side of the aisle and closets or cabinets are located on the other. The major disadvantage of this arrangement is that your bathroom is very narrow and usually no wider than the shower. This makes it difficult to use the bathroom for a dressing area unless you are a small person. However, it does have two major advantages. One is that it permits passage from the front to the rear of the coach and into the bathroom with complete privacy. The second is that it gives you a great deal of closet space across the aisle from the bathroom. My own coach is set up so that you can open both closet doors across the aisle to effectively create a private front and rear section of the coach with the intermediate bathroom. This would be a good arrangement if you have children or guests, if you plan to use your bedroom for a sitting area during the day, or if you need a lot of closet space.

Next is the side-aisle arrangement. The aisle from the galley to the rear bedroom is at one side of the coach. This has the distinct advantage of giving you a double-width bathroom that can also be used as a dressing area. However, you lose all that closet space across the aisle. Actually, you still have some closet space that can be built into the area adjacent to the shower since you probably will not expand your shower to the full width of the bathroom.

What this goes to prove is that you have only so many square feet to work with inside the coach and what you take for one thing must come from somewhere else. The professional conversion firms have little tricks based on past experience, but the bottom line is that you never have enough storage space and space utilization is a major factor in interior planning.

Actually, the side aisle arrangement is a good compromise since you have the ability to pass from the front to the rear of the coach while still retaining complete privacy in a bathroom that is large enough to serve as a dressing area. It is a good arrange-

ment for coaches that generally carry more than two people, particularly if you can find closet space elsewhere.

The latest development in bathroom configurations is intended primarily for couples. It has a center aisle but offers a full-width bathroom, usually with some substantial closet or storage space on one side. The major advantage of this arrangement is that it gives you a substantial dressing area. Its major disadvantage is that it prohibits passage from the front to the rear of the coach while the bathroom is in use. This may not be a major problem for a couple who use their back room for nothing more than a bedroom.

Most converted coach bathrooms contain a sink, a mirror or medicine cabinet, some cabinetry for storage and a shower. Some get more elaborate with a circular shower or a small Jacuzzi. A vent is frequently helpful. I might also suggest that some means of heating the bathroom is desirable since it can get cold at night if the door remains closed.

Next to the bathroom, your rear bedroom offers the most potential for individual expression. There are really only two major configurations although several variations are possible. One configuration involves twin beds, one placed on each side of the coach. Headboards are usually to the rear although they can also be placed toward the front. The other alternative is one large bed, which can be queen size if you have one of the newer, wider coaches or work your interior properly. With a single large bed you have a multitude of variations including both a rear and a front headboard and the island style with walkways on both sides. Some of the newer coaches place the bed sideways with the headboard on one side of the coach.

Preceding Page: **Custom Coach Corp. developed their ingenious Q/C (quick change) system to resolve that ongoing question of bedroom configuration. At night, you can have this island queen bed (above) which can also slide apart into twin beds at each side of the coach. During the day (below) the twin beds convert to couches, turning the rear bedroom into a travel lounge. This arrangement not only serves virtually every need but also can be used both at night and during the day.** © HIGH TIDES PHOTOGRAPHY/CUSTOM COACH CORP.

This determination of bed configuration has always been a major problem in both designing and in selling a coach. One convertor, Custom Coach Corp., has even developed a passable answer in what they call their Q/C for quick change bedroom. It provides twin couches on either side of the bedroom for daytime travel. At night they can be converted to twin beds. With a flip of a switch, they come together to create an island queen bed.

Any final determination on your rear bedroom should be based on whether you plan to use it during the day. Twin couches that make into twin beds will allow you to use the bedroom as a sitting or entertainment area during the day. This is a particularly good idea since a TV at the back will tend to bother the driver less than one in the front. Many coaches set up this way have a table that can be placed between the couches during the day

Individuals who do not use their coach for full-time living, have several smaller children, or want to use their bedroom during daytime travel, might be interested in the U-shaped rear lounge in the author's coach. With the table in place, it seats at least five adults and provides an excellent location for watching television or playing cards. At night, the table is removed and a center cushion put in place, creating a wall-to-wall bed for two adults or several smaller children. LARRY PLACHNO.

but removed at night. The twin bed idea also has some merit if you need more sleeping space since bunks can be placed above them.

The possibilities for other features in the bedroom area are almost limitless. Many coaches have a make-up table. My own coach has a small desk that converts into a make-up table when you lift the top. I have also seen coaches with an extra sink back there. If you have space, particularly if you plan to use this area during the daytime, you can include a chair or two. Closets, cabinets or drawers at either the front or the rear of the bedroom are typical as is a built-in TV or entertainment system.

In addition to the normal upstairs living area and bedrooms, I have seen converted coaches with either a bedroom or playroom for younger children built into one of the underfloor compartments. I personally dislike this arrangement since I do not feel it is safe for the children to be down there when the coach is

The rear lounge/bedroom in the author's coach has this interesting device created by Custom Coach. With the top in the down position, it serves as a handy small desk or writing table. However, with the top up (as shown) it becomes a make-up table complete with mirror and lighting. LARRY PLACHNO.

operating. Moreover, there tends to be a problem with the con-
flict between emergency exit and security. In most cases this question will not come up because most of us put so much equipment
into the underfloor compartments that there is no room remaining for any other purpose.

There is virtually no limit to the number of optional items that
can be included in a converted coach interior to meet the needs
and caprices of the coach owner. It would be impossible to list
them all but I can mention some of the more popular ones. In-

**Increasingly popular in converted coaches are these small combination
washer/dryer units. This one was installed in a new MCI shell by
Custom Coach and is hidden in its own cabinet. Immediately above
is a "garage" for galley appliances.** © 1991 HIGH TIDES PHOTOG-
RAPHY/CUSTOM COACH CORP.

creasingly popular is a small combination washer-dryer. Fold-down ironing boards and built-in galley appliances are popular. There is also an increasing amount of electronic equipment going into converted coaches including computers, elaborate entertainment systems, and even compact disk players. Most of the newer coaches do not have openable windows but they could be a big advantage on days with moderate temperatures and when parked at a campground. There are suppliers who provide openable windows with screens.

Beyond a simple lock on the front door, there are several options in the area of security. Many coach owners have a built-in safe for cash or valuables. Various types of security systems are also available and can be as elaborate as motion detectors and remote monitors.

The coach exterior should be briefly mentioned. Exteriors are usually painted although the colors and paint scheme are totally up to the discretion of the coach owner. Several different brands of good paint are available. DuPont's Imron is usually considered the best but it is among the most difficult and expensive to apply. Some coach owners go beyond the concept of conventional exterior paint schemes and have artists paint murals of favorite scenes or objects on the sides of their coach. In addition to the usual antennas, many coaches will have skylights or vents. Another typical addition to the exterior is docking lights on both sides of the coach to facilitate parking in campgrounds and parking lots after dark. If you plan to spend a great deal of time relaxing around your coach, you might consider a retractable awning. In addition, many converted coach owners pull a tow car or trailer and have a hitch and electrical connections at the rear for this purpose.

3

Converted Coach Systems and Components

While the previous chapter explored the various possibilities with converted coach interiors, this one will concentrate on the various systems and components that make such an interior workable. One of the major reasons why intercity coaches have been so viable as conversion shells is that their extensive underfloor compartments, originally intended for luggage and package express, serve very nicely to house the major components necessary for converted coach systems. This tends to place most of these components out of sight, and frequently out of mind, when in fact they are a major factor in good coach conversions. Following are the major systems that are worth looking into.

The first system you should consider is house heating. This can be considered the key system in most conversions since your decisions as to the type of heat you want and the type of energy you plan to use will have an impact on the other systems as well as on your interior design and appliances. There are three primary types of heating used in converted coaches although combination systems using two of them are not unknown.

In earlier days, virtually every RV and converted coach was equipped with propane for heating. It has several advantages including being clean burning, it requires minimal electrical power

Preceding Page: **Most converted coach system components are installed in the underfloor compartments. Unfortunately, this tends to keep them out of sight and frequently out of mind when they are very important to the overall operation of the coach. Shown are two underfloor compartments on an MCI converted by Custom Coach Corp. which include a large house battery system, other electrical components and air conditioning.** © 1991 HIGH TIDES PHOTOGRAPHY/CUSTOM COACH CORP.

for its use, and it is generally easily available at campgrounds and RV supply centers. If carried on the coach, propane can also be used for cooking or to power a refrigerator. The two most frequently heard complaints about propane are that it requires yet another supply item to be purchased and carried along and it requires safety considerations.

Proponents of propane point out that it is one of the least expensive heating systems to install and that it can be safe if you use the proper precautions. Opponents indicate that propane is illegal in several tunnels and is often either the primary cause or a contributing factor in converted coach fires and explosions. As a result many converted coach owners, myself included, do not feel safe in carrying propane on board. Today, propane is still used on many of the lesser expensive conversions but tends to be rather less used on the more expensive units.

Due to a combination of concerns for propane safety and developments in electrical components, the all-electric coach became popular about two decades ago and has continued to enjoy substantial popularity. Some major advantages of electric heat are that it is the cleanest heat source, it requires almost no maintenance, and it does not require purchasing or carrying along any additional energy source. Unlike other heat sources, electrical heaters are relatively easy to install since they come in various shapes and sizes and require only wires to make them work. They are also very easy to control with a thermostat and coach zone heating is very easy to arrange.

The only major drawback of electrical heat is its power requirements. For all practical purposes, battery systems cannot supply sufficient power for electrical heating for any prolonged period. Hence, you are highly dependent upon an auxiliary generator, or campground or shore power of sufficient quantity. With a 40-foot coach, 30 amps of regular a.c. household power may be adequate for a cool day but once the outside temperature drops below freezing, 50 amps is more appropriate and that is not available at many campgrounds. As a consequence, electric heat is practical for coaches that often use their generators at remote locations or frequent better campgrounds with good power supplies. If your situation is different, you may still wish to consider electric heat as a secondary system.

The latest trend is toward a heater fired by diesel fuel. This is not quite as clean as propane and may require some periodic maintenance but it has the advantage of using an energy source already on board the coach. In addition, the power requirements for such a system are small enough as to be in the range of many battery systems for a few hours of use. Hence, it can be a viable heating alternative even for remote locations.

Several different devices are available including the traditional Espar and a new unit offered by Thermo King. One of the newest is the Aqua Hot system developed by a company in Colorado. It uses diesel fuel to heat hot water that can then be used to heat the coach interior, even on a zone basis. The same device can also heat domestic water for showers and your hot water taps as well as heat a cold engine for ease of starting. This has become increasingly popular on more expensive conversions and even some less expensive conversions in recent years since it provides a good intermediate to the propane and electric systems.

A brief note should be made regarding the philosophy behind selecting heating systems. There are conversion owners called ''snow birds'' who go south in the winter and others who rarely drive north of the Mason-Dixon line. Many of these people have little interest in a sophisticated heating system. As a result, there are numerous converted coaches that are under-heated. Most of the experts recommend that a coach be provided with an adequate heating system if only for resale purposes or for those rare occasions when the coach finds itself in unseasonably cold weather.

There is some discussion regarding the retaining of the normal heating system that comes with the coach. It has the advantage of using the excess heat from your engine to heat the coach interior while going down the road. Its cost of operation and maintenance is minimal if it has already been installed. The biggest disadvantage is that the coach interior must be planned around the existing heating ducts and returns in order to leave it in place. Some people with an RV background tend to rip it out. I side with the commercial coach people in leaving it in since it eliminates the problem of turning on some other heating system while the coach is going down the road. A good criteria to use is that if you plan to do a lot of driving, the coach heating system is a definite advantage. If you expect to do less driving, the coach heating system may still be an advantage if it can be worked into your interior plans without major problems.

Over and above the normal interior heating, there are two other heating locations that should be considered on every coach. One is engine heating. Diesel engines tend to be difficult to start when cold and consequently most converted coaches provide some system or device to get the coolant warm so that they will start easily. The cheapest of these is the installation of an electric block heater. It has the advantage of easy installation and can easily be controlled by a simple switch on your master control panel.

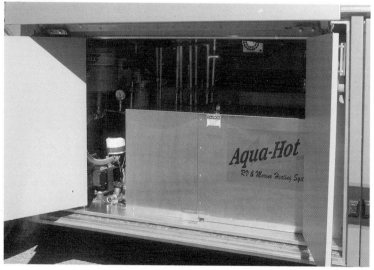

There is a recent trend toward using a diesel fuel fired system for house heating. This MCI converted by Custom Coach Corp. has an Aqua Hot system installed which not only heats the coach interior but also provides heat for domestic hot water, heating the underfloor compartments and heating the engine. Other diesel fuel fired systems are also available. © 1991 HIGH TIDES PHOTOGRAPHY/CUSTOM COACH CORP.

Its two disadvantages are that it is yet another drain on electrical energy and usually requires several hours to become effective. Most coach owners simply leave their block heaters on overnight if they need them. The other alternative is a fuel-fired heater for heating your engine coolant. This tends to be more expensive and is often connected with the house heating or domestic hot water systems.

The second area that requires heating in cold weather is your underfloor compartments, at least the one that contains your water tanks. If you have retained your coach heat, you are in luck because your coach heat ducts are probably already connected to this compartment and only require a little enlargement to be more effective. For heating while the main engine is not running, you can use either a small electrical heater or heat from a fuel-fired heating system if you have one.

Any discussion about air conditioning must take into account the fact that there are presently several changes underway in the refrigeration and cooling industry in regard to the chlorofluoro-carbons currently used as refrigerants. The former popular refrigerants have been shown to deplete the earth's ozone layer and are presently being phased out and replaced by newly-developed refrigerants. This change is far from being completed and regardless of what you do, you can look forward to some changes or modifications to your air conditioning system, and possibly your refrigerator, in the years ahead. Although there are variations, there are really only two basic types of coach air conditioning.

People with an RV background tend to have simple roof-top air conditioners installed. They are relatively easy to install and easy to hook up. Their two major disadvantages are that they tend to detract from the exterior lines of the coach and are prone to have a localized cooling effect. This last problem can be solved to a large extent by putting in some ducting. I personally have an aversion to cutting holes in a roof that may be highly stressed and part of the monocoque construction although problems from this have apparently been minimal.

Many people from the commercial side of the business and many of the leading conversion firms go with underfloor compressor units with refrigerant lines going to and from individual blowers in the interior of the coach. This type of system tends to be more expensive than the roof-top units but does detract less from coach appearance and seems to do a better job of cooling an entire area or room.

One suggestion I might make is that placement of the air conditioning units makes quite a difference. A single standard air conditioning unit may be adequate for the average rear bedroom. However, because of size, sunlight through the windows and air entering when the front door is opened, the front living and galley areas may require double this amount of air conditioning. Having insufficient air conditioning in the front of the coach is a typical conversion problem. The hallway and bathroom area rarely re-

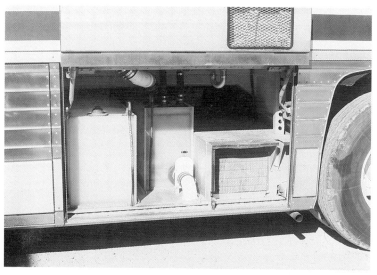

Converted coach water systems are generally relatively simple. Shown on the author's coach are two plastic tanks for fresh water (left) and black water (right). The pump and filter for the fresh water are located on the other side of the compartment. That large white pipe leading under the coach provides a connection for the three-inch flexible hose for campground dump stations. LARRY PLACHNO.

quires a separate unit if one or more of your other air conditioning units blow in that direction.

Finally, there is the question of whether to leave your coach air conditioning system in place or rip it out. Back in the early days when PD4104's had a separate air conditioning engine, it was typical for the RV people to rip it out because it was simply too difficult to maintain as a separate system. In more recent times, there has been a trend toward leaving the coach air conditioning in and operational. As with coach heat, it means one less thing for your conversion systems to cope with as you drive down the road.

Water and plumbing systems are relatively easy to understand and there are really only two major systems in use on converted coaches. One system involves two underfloor tanks: one for fresh water and one for black or sewer water. The other system simply adds a third tank for holding grey water from the sinks and shower. The advantage of the third tank is that grey water can be disposed of easier than sewer water and can also be used to flush out the black water tank. Differences between the two systems are more a matter of personal preference than outside factors.

In the standard system, water is taken from the fresh water tank by a small pump and usually is passed through a filter. The hot water line is then split off and routed through a hot water heater. Some of the more expensive coaches actually use separate lines from the underfloor compartment to each water tap and have individual shut-off valves. Return lines from the sinks and toilet work by gravity and are usually fitted with traps to reduce odors coming back into the coach. I have seen most of the normal household piping materials used in coaches but all must be constructed so that they do not easily come apart due to road vibrations. In spite of the traps, most converted coach owners use a chemical in their holding tanks to hold down the smell unless they are in a position to dump their sewer water every 48 hours.

Campground hook ups are relatively easy to understand. The conventional campground dump station requires a standard three-inch flexible hose, usually near the left rear of the coach. For most coaches and campgrounds, gravity alone is sufficient to carry the effluent from the holding tank to the dump station pipe. Some converted coach owners install a pump that not only moves the effluent along but also chops it into small pieces. However, most converted coach owners report that pumps are not really necessary since chemicals and movement of the coach tends to liquify anything in the black water tank in a relatively short period of time. Some of the coach owners with three tanks have a valve system that allows them to flush out their black water tank with grey water as they are dumping. There normally is a requirement that the holding tank outlet on your coach be capped

The right rear underfloor compartment on the author's coach contains the water system. From left to right are an air conditioning unit with the central vacuum unit above it, in the center is the black water tank while on the right is a hot water heater, water pump, water filter and the fresh water tank behind these. Incoming fresh water in a garden hose can come through a small hole in the floor and be connected to the piping, or it is sometimes easier just to fill the fresh water tank. Incidentally, that big handle next to the black water tank opens a valve for dumping at commercial bus garages, which have open dumps on the right. LARRY PLACHNO.

when operating on the highway. Most of these pipes, fittings and valves are easily obtainable at an RV supply store.

Campground fresh water is usually supplied from a standard garden hose outlet at the left rear of the coach. Some campgrounds take advantage of the flexibility of a garden hose connection and locate these outlets elsewhere; such as shared by two or even four campsites. The normal procedure is to hook the garden hose into your water system beyond your pump with a valve and connector arrangement. When connected, water pressure in the pipe will force the water through the garden hose and then through the pipes in your coach. It is just like being at home. The only problem I have with the system is that you need some really good washers and connectors on your garden hose to keep it from dripping and leaking at the connections. All converted coaches are also set up with a simple plug or valve system so you can fill your fresh water tank directly from the garden hose.

I would suggest that you use some caution in regard to your fresh water. Many converted coach owners use a great deal of discretion in regard to where they take on fresh water. Others use chemicals or special filters to purify the water or do not use the water for drinking unless first boiled.

The size and construction of the tanks can vary considerably from coach to coach. My own tanks are a type of heavy plastic but I have seen other materials used including stainless steel. The smallest tanks I have seen were about 50 to 60 gallons while some people who spend a great deal of time in remote areas have opted for tanks in excess of 200 gallons. A size of about 100 to 120 gallons per tank for a two-tank system seems to be typical.

The most complex system on a converted coach is undoubtedly the electrical equipment. Systems vary substantially from coach to coach if only because a wide range of different component options is now available to suit individual needs and tastes. One word of caution, however, if you are not an expert in electrical items, it is recommended that you leave the construction and installation of such a system up to an expert in this field.

Most converted coaches have either two or three battery systems. The basic coach battery system comes with the coach shell and is used primarily for starting the coach and for supplying electricity for the various interior and exterior lights. It normally consists of either two or three conventional large 8-D batteries and will be set up for either 12-volt or 24-volt d.c. power depending on which one your coach uses. The experts recommend that these batteries not be used for other purposes but be protected so that they will always be available to start and operate your coach.

Converted coaches also have a house battery system to handle the electrical needs of the conversion components. Experts recommend deep-draw batteries for this purpose but the actual number used varies substantially depending on both the needs of the owner and the needs of the coach. Many coaches are set up so that both 12-volt d.c. and 24-volt d.c. can be drawn from this system. Some coaches also have a small third battery system

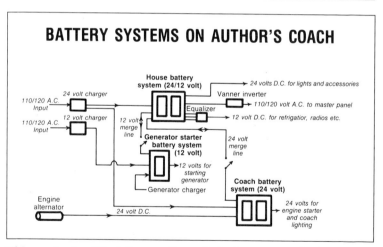

BATTERY SYSTEMS ON AUTHOR'S COACH

This overly simplified diagram shows the battery systems in the author's coach. The overall design with three battery systems and merge lines is typical of many converted coaches. This particular arrangement is manually controlled and very simplistic, whereas many of the newer conversions have gone to automatic switching devices. DRAWING BY DEB BARRON/NATIONAL BUS TRADER.

which exists primarily to start the auxiliary generator. The basic reason for having such a third system is to again keep it separate in order to insure that power is available to start the auxiliary generator.

There are at least four ways I know of to provide electrical input into the coach system.

The first of these is your engine alternator which provides d.c. power to charge your coach batteries while the engine is running. Newer coaches have such large alternators that they usually provide an excess of power that can be used for other purposes. Typical is a merge line or isolator that permits this excess energy to also charge the house battery system while the engine is running. If you then put an inverter on your house battery system, you have an excellent source for on-board 120-volt a.c. power while the engine is running. This, coupled with retaining coach heat and coach air conditioning, allows use of most coach features while the engine is running without having to resort to an auxiliary generator or draining your batteries.

A second source of power is a land line, which is actually little more than an extension cord, for use at campgrounds and other locations. On the larger and newer coaches, this is set up with a four-prong system to accept 50-amp, 240-volt power that is then brought into the main coach electrical panel as two 50-amp, 120-volt "legs." Inexpensive adaptors are easily available to convert the 50-amp plug to a 30-amp or 20-amp plug if that is all a campground has to offer. Most coaches have at least one battery charger so that batteries can be charged when the coach is connected to campground or shore power.

A third source for power is an auxiliary generator. This is most typically used when parked at a remote location when the main engine is not running and no connection is available for a land line. Generators can be either gasoline- or diesel-powered and can be either air cooled or water cooled. Diesel generators are becoming more popular because they do not need a separate, and admittedly more dangerous, fuel supply. The water-cooled units tend to be quieter. There is a wide range of sizes in use on converted coaches. Many of the older coaches have smaller generators that provide up to 5 kw or 8 kw in power. Newer coaches have had generators installed that provide up to 16 kw, probably gross overkill for most coaches in regard to power requirements. My own generator provides 12.5 kw and has proven to be more than adequate for all my remote electricity needs including electric heat. Auxiliary generators are usually set up so that they can also feed power into chargers for the battery systems.

Relatively new in the industry is roof-top solar panels. They do not offer a great deal of electricity, but what they do provide is apparently helpful in keeping batteries charged. In addition,

This 14.5 kw Kohler diesel generator was installed in an MCI conversion by Custom Coach Corp. In addition to having a pneumatically-assisted roll-out rack for service, it also has a roof-mounted exhaust.
© 1991 HIGH TIDES PHOTOGRAPHY/CUSTOM COACH CORP.

they require very little in the way of maintenance. Figures vary but some people insist that their solar panels will provide up to 10 amps of power on a sunny day, which is a big help in keeping batteries charged. Solar panels are still somewhat rare at this time but I expect them to become increasingly popular in the future.

It might be noted that there are presently two significant trends in the areas of a.c. and d.c. usage. The newer and more expensive coaches are going more and more toward increased use of a.c. power including full-size refrigerators, washer/dryers, and additional household appliances. This creates a need for ever-larger auxiliary generators and battery systems since most camp-grounds do not presently have sufficient electric service for these coaches. On the other hand, some of the converted coach owners who do a lot of remote camping are concentrating more on d.c.

Shown is the master electrical control panel on the author's coach where, in keeping with tradition, it is located above the driver's head and to the left. The top row of gauges represents a voltmeter for incoming AC power, two battery condition gauges, a thermometer and three gauges for the auxiliary generator. The smaller gauge on the second level measures a.c. current usage while the big switch on the bottom selects the type of a.c. input desired (land line, generator or inverter). LARRY PLACHNO.

equipment and larger battery systems. In addition to the previously available d.c. refrigerators, you can now obtain fluorescent lights, televisions and other appliances that operate from d.c. power. A coach set up this way can survive for long periods without a.c. power except for air conditioning.

Obviously, some means of controlling and selecting these various electrical options is necessary. The traditional means of doing this has been a large electrical control panel above the

Newer conversions planned to be used by only a couple have gone to placing electrical controls around the coach instead of solely in the driver's area. This modern control panel was recently installed by Custom Coach Corp. in a new MCI coach. It is hidden by a door and located in the galley area. © 1991 HIGH TIDES PHOTOGRAPHY/CUSTOM COACH CORP.

driver's head to the left or front. Design of the panel varies greatly depending on the coach and owner. Typical is a master switch for selecting generator, inverter or shore power; individual switches for the various components and circuits, and the desired meters and gauges. The advantage of such an arrangement is that it gives the driver complete control of the various systems and electrical components. The disadvantage is that the arrangement, if totally manual, is not fail-safe. An individual could easily leave a merge line connected between two battery systems and find that both have been drained to the point where they are useless. In addition, components could be easily damaged if you attempt to charge a battery system from two different sources.

Some of the newer coaches have gone to a more automatic or distributed electrical system. Electrical components now exist to automatically turn on battery chargers or merge lines when power is available. Switches are available to temporarily merge

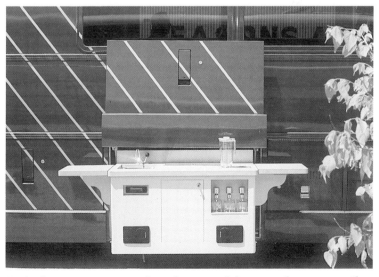

Underfloor compartments have been used for several purposes other than housing coach systems. Coaches used for outdoor entertaining have been equipped with underfloor equipment for both entertaining and cooking. This pull-out unit with a fold-out top was built into an MCI shell by Custom Coach Corp. LARRY PLACHNO.

two or more battery systems when starting the coach. It is even possible to have your auxiliary generator come on automatically when there is a power failure. In addition, some of the newer coaches, particularly those that are converted for the sole use of a couple, have gone into a less centralized electrical control system with smaller panels located around the coach. Although this has the disadvantage of permitting additional access to the controls, the convenience to the coach owner is obvious.

One other minor system is worthy of comment. Some coaches have a central vacuum system. It not only makes cleaning easier within the restricted confines of a coach but also eliminates the need to carry and move a vacuum cleaner, although you still need a hose and the end utensils. Installing the system is relatively simple since our experience is that only three inlets are necessary in a 40-foot coach.

Some converted coach owners make a particular point of having their campground connections both neat and well organized. A case in point is this left rear compartment on a Prevost converted by Marathon. In addition to offering a spotless environment for the connections, it also provides a supply of gloves and running water to keep the coach owner clean. Incidentally, those valves at the top are the shut -offs for each individual water line inside the coach. LARRY PLACHNO.

There are several different options available for remaining space in the underfloor compartments. Some portion of one of the underfloor compartments should have space for extra fluids and supplies. Some people keep a freezer in one of their underfloor compartments. Many converted coach owners try to keep one compartment totally open for extra luggage, guest luggage and other items they wish to carry along. This compartment is often carpeted. Some people like to have an extra water tap in one of the underfloor compartments so that you can wash your hands without coming inside when hooking up at campgrounds or working on the coach. Some people who do a lot of entertaining outside have an entertainment center built into one of the underfloor compartments. This often includes a TV and sound system but can also extend to some cooking facilities.

4

Converted Coach Operations

A private coach is not the same as an automobile. This has both its good and bad features. Regardless of what type of coach you acquire, you will invariably find yourself doing things differently with a coach than with an automobile. Most private coach owners easily adopt to these changes and automatically develop two different sets of criteria and habits depending upon which vehicle they are driving at the time.

Licensing and Insurance

Licensing and insurance normally represents no particular problem with a converted motorhome coach. In many states, a private coach is treated the same as a regular RV if it meets the stated criteria. Although some states are known to charge a relatively high fee for license plates, most provide licensing at a nominal fee. Insurance is available from several sources. The annual fee for a coach used exclusively for private transportation will generally not exceed the annual fee for a private automobile based in the same community. If you use your coach for commercial purposes or for transporting an entertainment group, you can expect to pay higher insurance rates. It is recommended that you insure your coach for a sufficient amount since there have

Preceding Page: **Converted coaches can make use of many overnight stopping places. Shown is the author's coach at the RV Resort and Yacht Club at South Padre Island, Texas, one of several operated by Outdoor Resorts of America. In addition to a double-width concrete parking pad, the campsite had water, a dump station and 50-amp electrical power.** LARRY PLACHNO.

been problems where replacement cost exceeded what the owner expected.

Driving

Past experience with training commercial coach drivers shows that the two most important features of a coach to learn beyond the switches, gauges and controls, are the shifting and turning.

Most larger intercity coaches built in the United States between 1950 and 1980 had a four-speed mechanical transmission with the shift in a standard "H" pattern and with reverse in the second gear position (left, down) after pressing a button. Other transmissions came into use after 1980, particularly a five-speed. With very few exceptions, coaches built in the United States and Canada do not have a synchromesh transmission. In plain English, this means that you not only have to double clutch between gears (place the transmission in neutral, release the clutch and then put it in again) but must also coordinate your engine and transmission speed to achieve a smooth shift. When downshifting, it is usually necessary to increase your engine rpm's in neutral before going into the next lower gear. It sounds fine in theory but can be a difficult skill for some people to acquire; even some professional drivers will occasionally "miss a gear." Many a novice coach driver has left a trail of transmission teeth on the road (possibly useful if you forget the way home) or has instilled something less than complete confidence in family members and friends riding along. Patience and a little bit of thought before action are highly recommended. If all else fails, find an excuse to spend several days practicing your shifting before carrying passengers.

Personally, I prefer stick shift over an automatic transmission, particularly in hilly country. But, like many other converted coach owners, both of my last two coaches were equipped with an automatic transmission. Automatic transmissions were virtually unheard of in intercity coaches prior to the 1970s. They have been retrofitted on a few older private coaches but only with significant expense.

Automatic transmissions are becoming more and more popular among converted coach owners. One reason is that an increasing number of converted coach owners have little experience with mechanical transmissions and none with the non-synchro variety. A second reason is that the automatic transmission will permit other family members and friends to drive the coach if you desire and encourage this.

Incidentally, if you opt for an automatic transmission, I recommend that your coach be equipped with a retarder for operating through hills. I personally prefer the Telma magnetic retarder because of its controlability, but the Jacobs Engine Brake (Jake Brake) is also recommended while a built-in transmission retarder also has some merit.

Turning is the second most important training point for new drivers. A 40-foot coach does not have the same turning radius as an automobile and ignoring this fact usually leads to dents, dings and other embarassing customized marks along the side of the coach.

Standard procedure calls for "squaring off" your turns by going farther into the intersection and then turning the steering wheel more sharply than you would in an automobile. For the novice, it is recommended that you execute difficult and sharp turns slowly and keep one eye on the appropriate external rear-view mirror to check the location of nearby curbs, vehicles and other obstacles.

Some professional drivers make turns look easy. One reason is experience but the other is a little trick known as thinking ahead. If there is more than one way to get into an area or to make a turn, the professional driver will take the safest route. If there is no choice, the professional driver will take extra care to position the coach so as to have the maximum leeway possible.

Backing up is generally considered to be one of the most dangerous and difficult maneuvers for a coach because vision is obscured to the rear. Always get out and personally inspect the area and obstructions prior to backing. If possible, have a passenger step outside to guide you. Many of the more recent converted coaches are equipped with a back up camera on the rear that puts the scene on a TV monitor at the driver's position. This has apparently been very useful for many coach drivers and is becoming increasingly popular.

Overhead clearances for buses are generally not the problem a newcomer might imagine. Although tall in comparison to automobiles, most buses are two feet shorter than the taller trucks. With only a very few exceptions, buses built in the United States and Canada do not exceed a height of 12 feet. I have yet to find an overpass on an interstate highway that will not clear a conventional bus. Hence, it can be said that a conventional bus will generally not encounter clearance problems unless you leave the main highways. However, it should be noted that most converted coaches are taller than their commercial counterparts because of additional equipment on the roof. A good policy is to have the height of your particular coach accurately measured and place a placard of some type on the dash so that you and other drivers will be aware of the actual height.

I have never had to back up because of a low viaduct but I once had a close call. The summer of 1990 found me going through Pierre, South Dakota with three of my children. I elected to eschew the posted truck by-pass route and take the state route through the city to see more of the town. Following the posted route, I made two quick turns and found myself facing a railroad viaduct with a posted height of less than 12 feet. Because of a TV antenna dome on the rear roof, my coach slightly exceeds 11½ feet in height. I eased the coach very gently through the underpass while one of my sons stood on the curb with a discouraging expression while watching for pending disaster and motioning me to slowly come ahead. As it turned out, we cleared the underpass by about two inches. However, we provided a good show for some passers-by, and I have since resolved to use more discretion when leaving the major highways and truck routes.

Considerably more of a problem, and frequently an outright hazard, are unmarked clearances. These include tree limbs, overhangs on fast food restaurants and motel canopies. Most of these are not marked and are often found on private roadways. Some coach drivers insist that they jump out and snare an unsuspecting coach. The sad truth is that they *are* unexpected. They are bad enough when encountered directly but present even more of a hazard when adjacent to the coach and hence out of sight and out of mind. A quick turn in the wrong direction can easily lead to an unexpected dent in the roof. This is one instance where you would have wished that you had taken the time to walk around the coach and look for potential problems and hazards before driving off.

Hills can present some particular problems for coaches in several areas. Particularly if you have a mechanical transmission, you will have to make a conscious effort to avoid "lugging" your engine on hills. Running your engine at too low an rpm while expecting it to put out more power for hill climbing can cause severe internal damage. The traditional way of avoiding this is to downshift to the next lower gear when your speed and engine rpm's start to fall off significantly. This keeps your engine at

Low clearances on private roadways, particularly if unmarked, are often more of a hazard than clearances on state and federal highways. Shown is the author's coach emerging from under the canopy at the Holiday Inn in Bridgeport, New Jersey. For the record, the coach cleared the overhead canopy with several inches to spare. LARRY PLACHNO.

higher rpm's although your speed will diminish. On particularly severe hills, you may have to downshift again.

In spite of what you hear, most bus engines will experience an increased operating temperature when climbing hills. This is particularly true of older buses and in hot, summer weather. I once owned a coach that had a real penchant for overheating on hills and shutting down automatically, particularly in hot summer weather. This tended to irritate the drivers, but most were eventually able to avoid the worst of the overheating with a little training. The overheating problem can be diminished to a large extent if you pay more attention to your tachometer. As strange as it may sound, your coach will run better and cooler through the hills if you keep your engine rpm's high. With higher rpm's you not only increase the cooling effect but the engine tends to overheat less from strain because it is putting out more power. For this reason, I often override my automatic transmission and kick it into a lower gear because the automatic is too slow for my liking in downshifting on its own. My last two coaches, both equipped with Detroit Diesel 8V-71 engines, tended to climb hills best at about 1,700 or 1,800 rpm's. Your coach may be a little different and you may have to experiment a little. The system works for me since I have not had a coach overheat and shut down on me in years including a trip through the Black Hills in 110-degree temperatures.

To control your coach when coming down a hill, standard procedure calls for using the same gear you would use in going up the hill. However, some of the newer professional driving manuals suggest that even a lower gear may be necessary for some vehicles. Once again I might mention the value of a retarder, particularly if you do not have a mechanical transmission or if you do a lot of hill driving. A coach is a heavy vehicle and can be difficult to handle on steep hills, particularly for a novice. A retarder is good insurance for keeping a coach under control and is well worth the investment if it saves you a few gray hairs or worse.

I would be remiss if I failed to mention road surfaces, a particular problem area among novice coach drivers. Intercity coaches are heavy and require a good road surface for proper support. Interstate highways are best although most any paved road will do. Gravel on a hard surface is usually adequate, particularly for travel at low speeds. However, any non-paved surface, particularly when wet, should be suspect. I have long since given up counting the number of novice drivers who elected to take a short cut or accepted a less desirable parking spot and sunk into the mud up to their axle. When that happens, only time and a big tow truck will solve the problem, and the cost of the rig will be exceeded only by the volume of your embarassment.

On a similar note, I might mention that even if the surface is hard, wet grass or mud (or even ice) on an incline should be avoided. On several occasions I have seen coaches unable to get up even a very slight incline if it was particularly slippery.

Somewhat related is the concept of keeping your coach well under control on major highways so you can safely stop in the event of an emergency ahead. What you want to avoid is the necessity of having to make a decision about leaving the roadway in the event of an emergency. Your coach is simply too large, heavy and awkward to tiptoe through a drainage ditch and take off through a neighboring farm. Most attempts to try this, particularly at speed, end up severely injuring both the passengers and the coach. Hence, the safest course of action is to stay far away from possible trouble and slow well in advance of any problem on the road.

Operating Restrictions

You should note that coaches do have several restrictions that you normally would not think about when driving an automobile. However, they should be considered and kept in mind.

In many states, converted and private coaches are subject to different speed restrictions than automobiles or commercial buses. When driving a coach, you may find yourself reading the fine print on the speed limit signs in some states. Unfortunately, as far as examples are concerned, I can only remember the states I drive through on a regular basis. In Illinois, commercial coaches have a top speed limit on the interstate highways of 65 miles per hour (where permitted) while RV's are limited to 55 miles per hour. Ohio, the birthplace of the converted coach industry, actually lists private coaches on their speed limit signs and limits them to 55 miles per hour on the interstates. On the other hand, such states as Indiana allow all vehicles to go 65 miles per hour on the interstates (where permitted) and Ontario's major highways permit all vehicles to travel at a maximum of 100 kilometers per hour. Hence, two suggestions. One is that a coach driver must watch the speed limit signs more closely. The second is that I have found that I can actually cut a significant portion of travel time where alternate routes are available by selecting the state with the best speed limits. Incidentally, the speed limits mentioned above are examples only and subject to change, your speed should be guided by the actual signs along the road.

Coach drivers must also watch out for various weight restriction signs or postings. Most coaches are heavy enough to run afowl of both highway and bridge weight limits. This would rarely be a problem on interstate or state highways, but once you get off on secondary roads such restrictions are inevitable. Two types of roads come particularly to mind. Where a winter freeze is typical, many secondary or farm roads will be posted with lower weight restrictions in the spring. In addition, most side streets in major cities will have weight restrictions.

Commercial vehicles are prohibited the use of some roadways although most of these restrictions rarely pertain to private coaches. Nonetheless, if faced with two different routes around or through a town, the coach owner might wisely elect to take the truck route since it generally has the easier turns and grades. There are some restrictions on coach parking in private parking lots but these are usually posted. Many major municipalities also have restrictions on overnight street parking or on overnight RV parking in residential areas. If you plan to spend the night in the driveway or in front of a private home, you should take the time to ask about local ordinances.

Private coach owners should avoid carrying passengers or any type of freight on a commercial basis. In most cases, this is not permitted under the normal licensing and insurance for private coaches and RV-type converted coaches. It could cause you serious problems if it is discovered or if you are involved in an accident.

Different Types of Usage

With the noteworthy exception that they usually require a slower speed on curves, coaches are amazing vehicles. Because of their weight, they are more stable on the road and require less effort to drive. Most coach drivers report that they can drive more miles or more hours in a coach than in an automobile because it requires less effort.

What I find very interesting is the vast differences on how people use their coaches. Some of the retired "full timer" coach owners emphasize the "home" portion of their motorhome. They get up late, have breakfast at 9 a.m., unplug from the campground at 10 a.m., and spend four or five hours driving. By mid-afternoon, they are pulling into another campground for the night because they dislike driving or coming into a campground after dark. They may not cover many miles but they enjoy the amenities of their coach.

At the opposite end of the spectrum are those of us who use coaches for transportation and emphasize the "motor" portion of the motorhome. It is amazing how many miles you can cover in a coach if you keep moving. And with a coach you can keep moving because you have the advantage of driving ease coupled with on-board amenities and a relatively large operating range. I regularly knock off 600 to 650 miles in a 12- to 14-hour period without exceeding the speed limit. When I have to cover a lot of miles in one day, I hold stops to a minimum and keep one ear tuned to the CB radio to listen for weather conditions and hazards ahead. My other ear is usually tuned to my cassette player and my favorite songs. Unfortunately, I have a bad habit of singing along with the music which tends to drive my passengers to the rear of the coach so they don't have to put up with the awful noise.

Coaches and Bad Weather

There is virtually nothing negative that can be said about converted coaches and bad weather. Many newcomers to converted coaches think of them as fair weather vehicles because of previous experience with RV's. Others expect to be delayed frequently by bad weather. Neither expectation is correct. The first advantage of the converted coach is that it is self-contained. In the event that you encounter really bad weather, you can pull off the road most anywhere and survive very comfortably in your coach until the road is passable again. The second advantage of the converted coach is its excellent driveability. It is both heavier and higher than an automobile, and does not bend in the center like a truck. As a result, the coach has less of a problem with snow and is probably the most stable vehicle on the highway. To a large

Coaches do remarkably well in bad weather. They are not only more stable on the road than many vehicles, but converted coaches have the advantage of being able to stop most anywhere if the situation becomes hazardous. What is required is an experienced driver, proper safety precautions and reducing speed as necessary. ROBERT REDDEN/REDDEN ARCHIVES.

extent, its ability to handle bad weather is limited more by the experience of the driver than anything else.

Having many years experience in coach operations in the Midwest, and driving long distances year around, I have spent so many hours driving a coach in the snow that I take it as a relatively routine matter. In recent years, I have made a special effort to stock up on food and fuel when approaching an area of known storms and bad road conditions. Hence, if conditions really get bad, I will be in a good position to pull off the road and enjoy a forced vacation until the weather improves. Unfortunately, the weather rarely gets bad enough to warrant taking advantage of this.

To prove the driveability of coaches in snow, let me relay my own worst snow adventure. In spite of my own experience with commercial coach operation, this particular incident involved a converted MC-7 on a private trip to a Florida bus show in January of 1987. We started out just before dawn from our base in the Midwest and pointed the coach south using state highways. When we started, the sky was crisp and clear but less than an hour later, it started to snow. Within two hours of departure, we found ourselves in a heavy blizzard. We did have some discussion about stopping and taking alternate routes but since we were driving at a reduced speed, the coach was still stable and there appeared to be no immediate safety hazard.

The last stretch over the state highway (now being replaced by an interstate highway) was probably the worst. A blanket of snow covered the road to such an extent that it would have been virtually impossible to tell where the pavement ended except for the cars in the ditches. We contemplated stopping, but since we could not tell a good pull-off from a bad one, and since the coach was still stable in low gears, we continued slowly south. We did offer assistance to some of the automobile people and finally reached Bloomington, Illinois about an hour later than expected.

We took the ramp up to the interstate and soon found ourselves on a road of virgin white snow with absolutely no traffic. In making our way around Bloomington, we had the interstate to ourselves which produced a very eerie feeling. On at least two occasions we encountered drifts up to the height of the front bumper, the only time I have seen this on an interstate highway that was supposedly open to traffic. We would have stopped if the snow continued to be this high but it was lower as we went east. The coach continued to handle well at moderate speeds and we knew that the snow situation was better up ahead. We stopped once or twice to knock encrusted snow from the wipers and then continued east to Indianapolis. By the time we reached the Indiana state line, the snow had diminished considerably, plows were out, and we had company on the highway. We arrived in Chattanooga that night about two hours late. Along the way we discovered that the state highway and two of the interstates had officially been closed within minutes after we passed.

I should hasten to point out that this was not a typical private coach situation. The coach involved had been maintained to commercial standards, had been used by us for years, and was well equipped for winter operation. Moreover, the other driver on board and I had extensive commercial experience. Both of us had served as driver trainers and safety supervisors, and both of us had extensive snow driving experience, both in this coach and in others. Given the same situation with other coaches and drivers, I would recommend getting off the highway. However, this does show what a coach can do in the snow.

It is obvious that the experience of the driver has a great deal to do with the safety of the coach. Let me pass along another true story to put this into perspective.

Some friends of mine, who are commercial coach operators from Ontario, were driving south to a bus meeting. A freak snow storm had hit Atlanta, paralyzing traffic and closing roads. My friends encountered road blocks approaching Atlanta, but after talking to the officer in charge, they were able to get permission to continue on. The few inches of snow that was a disaster to local automobiles was an everyday event to professional drivers from the north.

Over the years I have come up with four situations where weather gets bad enough to warrant parking rather than carrying on.

1) Anytime you do not feel comfortably in control of your coach, it is time to park. This can include heavy fog as well as snow and ice.

2) Coaches do well in snow if you slow down, use common sense, take extra precautions and have the experience to handle the situation. However, it is time to park when you start pushing snow with your front bumper. Although the snow may still be driveable, you risk damage to the equipment under the floor when the snow gets this high.

3) Never drive on roadways covered with black or sheet ice. While they can survive other bad weather, coaches are particularly prone to slipping, and this is considered the worst of all road conditions by professional drivers. Black ice is usually localized and of relatively temporary duration so you may find an alternate route by listening to your CB radio, or you may accept a relatively short delay.

4) Consider stopping or other alternatives if the outside air temperature drops below zero degrees and your coach is not specifically prepared for cold weather operation. At normal highway speeds at that temperature, the wind chill on the underside of your coach can be the equivalent of 80 degrees below freezing. Frozen brake or air lines are possible and can be a disaster. Back during a particularly cold Midwest winter in the mid-1980s, I had a commercial coach freeze its lines while on an interstate highway in temperatures around 20 degrees below zero. This happened in spite of precautions like putting alcohol in the air lines.

Fuel and Supplies

Travel routine with a coach is substantially different than with an automobile. The most obvious change is that with an automobile you can stop at any convenient gas station. Bus engines are powered by diesel fuel which is not available at most conventional gas stations. As a result, most private coach owners will stop for fuel at truck stops. There are other alternatives such as bus and truck garages, but truck stops tend to be the easiest to find and most convenient.

As with gas stations, you have your choice of a wide range of brands of fuel as well as independent or chain ownership of the truck stop. Some private coach owners I know buy their fuel on price and look for the cheapest they can get. Having come from the commercial end of the business, I have an aversion to cheap fuel and simply do not trust it. Invariably, I will purchase my fuel from one of three nationally known brands or at least a truck stop tied in with the National Truckers' Service. As a result, I will pay a few cents more per gallon for my fuel, but I almost never have a problem with it.

Operations at truck stops are very similar to gas stations with perhaps two exceptions. Some truck stops either have an attendant meet you at the pumps to obtain information on your vehicle and method of payment, or they may expect you to verify credit before they turn on the pump. The other difference is that some truck stop pumps are set up for trucks, which generally prefer to fuel from the left side but often fuel from both sides. This occasionally creates minor problems for coaches, most of which fuel on the right side. If you have not seen it before, the most confusing situation is a secondary or slave fuel pump where you find a standard pump with readings on the left and a simple stand or hose without readings but with a matching pump number on the right. Their primary purpose is to permit a truck to fuel from both sides from one pump reading. There are two ways to cope with this situation. The easiest is to first turn on the master pump on the left, which may often also include removing the pump nozzle, and then you can fuel from the secondary or slave pump on the right. The second alternative is to enter the fuel island from the other side, although this may cause some confusion in traffic patterns and almost always will elicit some remarks from the neighboring truck drivers regarding the intelligence of coach drivers.

Many professional drivers will look for the presence of a fuel supply truck before pulling up to the fueling island and will go elsewhere if they see one. In many cases the new fuel being delivered, particularly if the underground tanks are small, will stir up sediment that will get into the fuel being pumped out.

Coach fuel stops tend to be more lengthy than automobile fuel stops if only because you are pumping more gallons of fuel. However, most private coach owners develop routines to shorten or make use of this time, and I find that I can often cut down fueling time to as little as 15 minutes. The most typical routine is to start the fuel flowing and then move to the front of the coach to clean the windshield. Most truck stops provide some type of stepladder and equipment for this. I carry my own stepladder and equipment if they do not. Then, having given the oil a chance to settle, you can go back to the engine compartment and check your oil level. However, I would suggest that you stick around the coach when fueling since some of those automatic shut-off devices on the fueling nozzles may malfunction from time to time.

Most experts recommend waiting 20 minutes after turning off your engine to check the oil in order to give it a chance to settle. This means that if you check your oil too soon at a truck stop, your oil dip stick may show a lower reading than the actual situation. The best time to check oil is in the morning before you start the engine, but I will check mine along the road if fueling, driving heavy, or driving through mountains. Two comments may be applicable in regard to oil levels. First, take care in inserting your dip stick because some have caps that can catch and cause an improper reading showing your oil level lower than is actually the case. The second is that with a Detroit Diesel engine I almost invariably run my oil level a little below the "full" mark. This still gives me a good margin for safety while reducing the wastage that gets blown out from overfilling and invariably ends up on the back of the coach.

I might note that in the event of an emergency, you can use the automotive diesel fuel sold in most gas stations. Some of this is of a better grade than found in truck stops and most of it is more expensive. However, it works fine and the better grades may even give you better mileage than the standard fuel from truck stops.

An often asked question by new coach owners is "when do I fuel?" The question has substantial merit since most commercial coaches, particularly the older ones, were built without a fuel gauge. What most coach drivers do is to develop a rule of thumb based on average fuel consumption and either miles or hours. If your fuel tank holds 150 gallons and you want to be safe and fuel when you need 100 gallons, and your average fuel consumption is six miles per gallon, then you fuel every 600 miles. I once had a coach that carried 179 gallons of fuel but had no fuel gauge. With that one we got so lax that we began fueling every day and a half unless we were driving hard. Regardless of what method you use, make sure that you leave a substantial margin for safety. Coach fuel systems are complex and pressurized. If you run out of fuel, you must reprime the fuel system to get it going again. This often requires calling out a mechanic with special equipment.

If you are new to diesel engines, I would be remiss if I did not bring up the subject of fuel "waxing." Most automobile drivers pay very little attention to the possibility of temperatures affecting their fuel. Diesel fuel is much more prone to this and must be carefully watched. Unless blended or treated with an additive, conventional diesel fuel can start to wax with temperatures as high as 40 degrees. In cold temperatures without additives, the paraffin will separate from the fuel and form a substance that looks like a white jelly. What it does is to block off your fuel lines and filters which will effectively cut off your fuel supply and cause your engine to shut down.

My own worst experience with this took place nearly 10 years ago. My family and I flew down to Florida late in the year to pick up a newly converted coach. I never thought about cold temperatures because it was warm enough for swimming, so I filled up with conventional fuel. We drove back home to the Midwest and parked the coach on the driveway. But the next morning we discovered that it had gotten so cold overnight that it had snowed. The coach started fine but only ran a few minutes before the wax shut off the fuel supply. It took us several days to get the coach running properly again since the best solution includes several days in a warm garage, new fuel filters and some fuel additive. Since then, I think ahead one or two fuel stops when determining outside temperatures and the need for blended fuel or additives.

In spite of notices on your coach suggesting the use of number one diesel fuel, most of the conventional diesel fuel sold at truck stops in 1991 is the lesser number two grade. I understand that some federal legislation is pending to improve this because of pollution problems. When temperatures drop, the better truck stops will sell a blend of number one and number two fuel to prevent waxing. Ask at the fuel desk if the pumps are not marked. You can usually count on this working provided you are not headed where temperatures are lower. In that case, or if you are not sure, the safe course is to purchase some anti-waxing fuel additive and put it into your tank before you fuel.

Most automobile drivers carry little or nothing in the way of spare fluids and supplies with them. However, either because of convenience or because of a lack of immediate availability on the road, most private coach owners allocate a corner of one of the underfloor compartments for this purpose. The amounts and type of fluids carried will vary according to the needs of the coach and the concerns of the coach owner.

Virtually everyone carries a few gallons of extra engine oil. Although easily obtainable at any truck stop, most of us tend to check and add oil in the morning before starting when we may be parked in a campground. I usually also carry a gallon of oil (different weight) for my auxiliary generator. Many coach owners carry anti-freeze or a 50/50 anti-freeze water mixture that can be used for coolant in either the main engine or auxiliary generator. At least one coach owner I know carries kerosene for use in thinning fuel, cleaning parts, washing the engine, and as a starting primer. Additions beyond this can include distilled water for the batteries, diesel fuel additive, transmission fluid, or engine starting fluid.

Some diesel engines show a real reluctance to start on cold mornings. The preferred means of getting them warmed up is either a fuel fired coolant heating system (if you have one) or several hours of operation of an electric block heater. Engine starting fluid must be used carefully since it can damage your engine, but it is the standard fall-back position if nothing better is available.

Where to Spend the Night

Those of you who have some prior experience with RV's already have some knowledge in this area. However, coaches are slightly different than most RV's because of size and power requirements.

Since coaches are so self-contained, you can spend the night virtually anywhere and some less-concerned coach owners take advantage of this. However, to avoid problems for yourself and other coach owners, I strongly suggest that you stay away from private property unless you have specific permission.

My favorite overnight stops are campgrounds. Most provide electric, water and sewer hook ups, a small grocery store and even a swimming pool, all for as little as $15 to $20 a night. It should be noted that quality can vary substantially from one campground to the next. There is at least one national chain and several in-

Several different coaches belonging to members of the Converted Coach Owners are lined up at the Indiana Beach campground during a rally in July of 1991. Most campgrounds will provide coaches with a camping site equipped with connections for electricity, water and a dump station. This particular campground also had several on-site activities including a water slide, miniature golf and an arcade. LARRY PLACHNO.

dependent resorts that cater to coaches and larger RV's with concrete pads and good power supplies.

There are some negative features to campgrounds. One is that they may be difficult to get into if you are on the road late at night. Some campground offices may close early in the evening and many private coach owners have an aversion to maneuvering in a strange campground after dark. Office hours may not be a major problem if you phone ahead since many campgrounds are willing to hold or assign a space on the phone and allow you to pay in the morning. Whether you want to try to find that space in the dark is up to you.

A second frequent campground problem is maneuverability. Most campgrounds are built for vehicles that are shorter than 40-foot coaches. However, except for those built on hills or in a forest, I have had few problems with a 40-foot coach if you take your time. My worst problem came in a campground in West Virginia where I had to back up nearly a quarter of a mile on a campground lane because my coach could not make a sharp turn ahead. On another occasion, I had problems making a turn on a narrow cliffside road leading to a hillside campground in upstate Pennsylvania. So far, both the coaches and I have survived but these campground problems do exist.

My own worst complaint about campgrounds is their electrical power. In addition to getting off the highway to a hopefully quiet area, my main interest in a campground is in obtaining an electrical hook up so I do not have to run my auxiliary generator. My current coach is all electric, and big coaches require a lot of power, particularly if you intend to run electric heat or air conditioning. Fifty amps (particularly if 240 volts) is delightful, 30 amps may be sheer survival in the summer and less in cold weather, while 20 amps is a joke. In many cases, particularly in the dead of winter, I find it more desirable to find a spot where I can run my auxiliary generator rather than try to survive on inadequate campground power. I might suggest that this is an excellent reason for having some type of fuel fired heating system if you expect to do a great deal of winter traveling and camping.

In addition to private campgrounds, there are numerous state and federal parks that offer camping sites. Most (but surprisingly, not all) provide fewer services than the average campground but compensate with lower fees.

There are a couple national campground guides available in larger bookstores that list these campgrounds and their facilities. Spending some hours studying alternatives, or phone calls to the campground management, is usually a good investment in selecting suitable stopping places before a trip. If you do phone the campgrounds, you should tell them you have a bus since there is a significant difference in wheel base and turning radius between a coach and a larger RV.

Those who travel with children and are used to automobiles and motels may find coaches and campgrounds a welcome alternative. Many campgrounds provide pools and other play equipment or attractions fully equal to motels. However, I find that

The author's coach is shown on a camping site at the Darien Lake Campground in New York. In spite of its location adjacent to an amusement park, we were able to reserve the site by telephone only a few hours in advance. Although not a pull-through site, it was easy to get into and did have water, a dump station and electric service. LARRY PLACHNO.

campgrounds have a decided edge in morning departures. At a motel, you spend at least an hour waking the kids, packing their things, getting them dressed, feeding them breakfast, and then carrying things to the car.

When I am planning an early departure from a campground, I put the younger children in the back bedroom of the coach and sleep up front. After the alarm clock rings in the morning, it only takes me 15 minutes to get dressed, unhook from campground facilities, count sleeping bodies without waking them, and make a cup of coffee. The basic philosophy is that if various belongings were on board the coach in the evening they will still be there in the morning, and their state of disarray makes no difference to coach operation. I can often be on the road and into the next state before they climb out of bed and start looking for breakfast.

Two other notes regarding campgrounds are applicable. One is that campgrounds have a decided advantage regarding showers. If remotely parked and operating solely off your water tanks, most coach owners tend to take a rather short shower in order to preserve water. However, if hooked into campground services you can enjoy a longer shower. The second is that coach operating cost (not necessarily including maintenance) plus campground fees is almost always less expensive than automobile operating costs plus motels.

If you are planning on driving until late at night, a truck stop can make a viable alternate to a campground. Most of the larger truck stops provide an overnight parking area for truckers that is relatively easy to get into after dark. Arrangements can vary since some charge no fee at all, others require that you purchase fuel and a few charge a parking fee. Advantages include a location adjacent to a main highway, the availability of services at the truck stop possibly including a grocery store and restaurant, a store with all kinds of things for trucks and coaches, and the probability that no one will complain if you run your auxiliary generator all night. Disadvantages include the lack of scenery, noise from the trucks, and the need to take extra safety precautions (particularly with children) when walking around the moving trucks.

Some private coach owners like to stay in highway rest areas but they have both good points and bad. Some states prohibit overnight parking, but these are often posted and there are lists available in some of the campground guides. A more pressing problem is that if you arrive late during a busy time of year, you may find all of the spaces already taken by trucks and other vehicles. You may find it necessary to run your auxiliary generator in hot or cold weather. The most frequently heard complaint is that highway rest areas can be noisy with traffic all night.

Private property can make a good overnight stop if you have permission. As long as local ordinances do not prohibit this, you can spend the night in the driveway of a friend or relative. However, it is recommended that you take extra precautions to avoid cracking concrete driveways or running over lawns and

Among the more interesting unofficial campgrounds on private property is this location adjacent to the Prevost Car bus manufacturing plant in Ste. Claire, Quebec. Prevost Car offers use of the sites to Prevost owners who come in for service or for potential Prevost owners who would like to tour the plant. The electric service provided puts most campgrounds to shame and the neighboring French-Canadian community is a delight to visit. LARRY PLACHNO.

shrubs. It may not hurt your coach but you could ruin a good friendship. Private and shopping center parking lots are questionable unless you have prior permission. Some parking lots are specifically posted that overnight parking is prohibited while others are well-known havens for RV and coach people. It is best to check if you are not sure.

Once you have some experience with coaches and develop some friendships, you will often discover lesser-expected overnight spots. For example, I have several friends who own bus companies and frequently spend a night in a bus garage parking lot. I have often also obtained permission to spend a night in a private parking lot belonging to a company when I had some business to transact in the morning.

One of the many advantages of converted coaches is that they can survive a night most anywhere if the location is suitable and permission is available. Shown is the author's coach spending a night in a parking lot at the Eagle Bus Manufacturing plant in Brownsville, Texas. LARRY PLACHNO.

Breakdowns, Maintenance and Parts

Because of both their larger size and specialized design, maintenance on coaches can be more of a problem than with automobiles. In fact, a conscientious private coach owner will probably spend at least as much per mile of operation in maintenance as will a commercial coach owner. Coming from the commercial end of the business, I am frequently appalled at the lack of attention many private coach owners pay to safety and maintenance. Admittedly, the extra time, care and expense necessary with a large vehicle is frankly one of the major negative aspects of coach ownership. However, given the proper procedures, the entire maintenance operation can be brought down to an easily understood and manageable level.

Many prospective and novice coach owners seem to have an inordinate fear of engine problems. Admittedly, the engine is easily the single most expensive component in most coaches. In 1991, a really good professional major overhaul on a typical bus engine can run close to $10,000, certainly a major expense for any coach owner. However, my experience is that most of these fears are misdirected. At the risk of paying a compliment to the people at Detroit Diesel, in spite of its complexity and what we ask it to do, the engine is easily one of the more reliable components on a coach.

Preceding Page: **The author's coach is parked adjacent to Executive Coach Corp. in Fox River Grove, Illinois. Conversion and specialized bus shops are good places to have private coach service and maintenance work done because they are familiar with the vehicles. They also have the skill, equipment and parts to do the job.** LARRY PLACHNO.

In spite of their complexity, engines tend to be one of the more reliable components on a converted coach. If properly cared for, they will give the private coach owner many years of dependable service. Shown is a high horsepower Detroit Diesel engine in an MCI shell converted by Custom Coach in 1991. LARRY PLACHNO.

My past experience is that a coach engine usually requires only four things to keep running properly. First, keep it supplied with good fuel. Second, keep it supplied with enough anti-freeze for the temperatures in which you are operating, and the proper corrosion inhibitors to keep the silicate level down. Three, keep it supplied with the proper engine lubricating oil. And, four, do not abuse it. This includes avoiding lugging the engine on hills, putting on the fast idle if you let it idle for more than a minute or two, and take care when using starting fluid. Given these criteria, the average Detroit Diesel engine in a private coach should provide at least 300,000 miles of use between major overhauls, and you may be able to stretch this to as much as 500,000 miles. Depending on circumstances, you may find it necessary to have the engine looked at periodically or have some components replaced, but these situations should be relatively rare if you take care of your engine. Most situations of failure of low-mileage engines are due to some lack of attention on the part of the coach owner or driver.

On-the-road coach problems are rarely so drastic. Typically, they are caused by the failure of an inexpensive component part but may require some time and expertise to locate and replace. Let me relate my own experience with on-the-road problems during a recent 12-month period that covered nearly 20,000 miles of coach operation.

My worst problem of the year was the blow-out of a front tire while approaching Memphis one evening in February. Tires are a very typical private coach problem since they usually warrant replacement because of age and weathering long before they wear out from mileage. In my situation, it only took a little more than an hour to get someone out to us at the side of the road to replace the tire with our spare. Unfortunately, we then discovered that the tire managed to take out the air brake line on that wheel when it went. Another four hours were spent in locating an all-night truck stop repair facility, waiting in line, and having the air line replaced. We did not reach our intended campground until after midnight.

Our second worst problem of the year came when our alternator belts decided to come apart on Goat Island in Niagara Falls, New York in August. That left us without power or coach air conditioning, neither of which was an immediate problem since we have an auxiliary generator. Although I carried spare belts, I elected to cross the river into Canada and had the belts replaced in a bus garage in about an hour.

Beyond that, all of our problems were minor. I replaced one headlight, the turn signal flasher and a few light bulbs. In addition, I had two light bulb pigtails put in. As a coach ages, the light socket pigtails tend to go bad with some frequency and I find it a good procedure, since the expense is minimal, to simply replace them rather than try to nurse them along.

All things considered, this is a relatively good showing for 12 months and 20,000 miles. However, I should point out that my coach is subject to relatively strict preventive maintenance procedures which involved replacement of other parts and components during this period.

There are three things you can do to reduce or minimize the impact of on-the-road coach problems. The first of these is a strict preventive maintenance procedure. Virtually all of the commercial coach operators have such a procedure because it is difficult to operate reliably without it. You will find it very helpful to institute your own version of such a procedure. Some details will be provided later.

A second suggestion is to think ahead and join one of the national breakdown services for coaches. There are at least three that I am aware of and I belong or have access to two of them. They typically will take emergency calls and then either dispatch someone to the site to do the work, if simple (such as tires), or have your coach towed to the nearest appropriate repair station. Hopefully, you will not need such a service very often but when you do, you will be happy that you have it. I might also note that most coaches can be severely damaged if lifted up off the highway for towing. For short distances, it is preferable to run an air line from the tow truck to the coach and then pull it while flat on the highway. For longer distances, a wheel lift unit or a flat-bed trailer is required.

The third item that helps is keeping some spare parts with you on the coach. This is rarely of significant help if you have a major problem, but a small parts supply can often turn a minor problem into nothing more than an inconvenience. What people carry along as spares usually reflects the particular nature of their coach and their own concerns. Most people who own coaches with 24-volt electrical systems usually carry spare headlights and other bulbs since they are not easily obtainable on the road and can usually be replaced in minutes by the owner. I usually carry replacement belts for both my engine compartment as well as my auxiliary generator. I also carry spare fuses for my conversion electrical system and spare filters for my conversion water system. For 10 years I have carried spare air bags for the coach suspension system but have yet to use one. Interestingly, I also carry spare garden hose washers because mine always seem to get lost from hooking up and unhooking at campground water supplies. Some people I know who have had fuel problems often carry spare fuel filters. Beyond that, anything else is optional if you have the space and the interest.

If you have a problem, either on the road or at home, a great deal of time and effort can be saved if you classify the problem. A converted coach is actually a composite of at least three or four different technologies. Where you go for help or parts depends on the appropriate group. I tend to classify these as truck, bus, conversion and general.

If your problem can be resolved at a truck stop, that would be your first choice if only because they are plentiful and easy to find. Typically in this group are tires and most engine and air line problems. Problems involving exclusive bus components can best be solved at a bus garage, a bus repair facility if you can find one, or at many of the conversion repair shops. Problems with conversion items are, fortunately, rarely safety-related and usually will not restrict operation. They fall into different categories. The more difficult ones may require the assistance of a conversion repair shop or an authorized repair service for that particular component or appliance. Simple things such as the pipes and hoses for dumping black water can be found at many RV stores. Finally, there are general items such as nuts, bolts and simple fixtures that can often be picked up at any hardware store and replaced by a competent individual.

Preventive Maintenance

Those who have never owned or operated heavy vehicles before probably have no real knowledge of preventive maintenance. Automobile owners know that they should take their vehicles in to their dealer or service station periodically for service. This is

There are several bus repair firms as well as service departments at some of the larger bus conversion firms that specialize in converted coach repairs and maintenance. Shown is a five-bay service area at Custom Coach Corp. in Columbus, Ohio where their trained staff provides complete maintenance, repairs and service on converted coaches. CUSTOM COACH CORP.

actually preventive maintenance on an automobile level although many automobile owners may not be aware of what is done and why it is done. Being both larger and more complex, a coach requires a more elaborate preventive maintenance program to accomplish the same things.

In simplistic terms, there are two ways to operate a coach. The first (and not recommended) way is to simply get in and drive it until it breaks down or a serious safety deficiency forces you to pull to the side of the road. You then fix the problem and go merrily on your way. The second way is to anticipate your problems before they become a safety hazard or cause a breakdown. This is the basic principle behind preventive maintenance. In addition to being recommended, it is usually both safer and less expensive in the long run than ignoring potential problems and waiting for things to happen.

The basic theory behind preventive maintenance is to find and fix a potential problem before it becomes an actual problem. Even if you do not now have a preventive maintenance program, you are already using this theory to some extent. A good example is your fuel tank. If you have a 136-gallon fuel tank, you probably stop for fuel when you can add about 100 gallons. There are two important aspects to this procedure. The first is that adding more fuel at this point prevents coach failure due to running out of fuel. The second is that fueling when you have room for 100 gallons represents an optimum point. You could stop more frequently and put in only 25 gallons, but this represents wasted effort. If you planned to stop when you could put in 140 gallons, you would run the risk of coach failure from a lack of fuel. However, stopping when you can add 100 gallons gives you a margin of safety while keeping effort to a minimum.

Your fuel tank is only one attention point on your coach. Depending on how critical you want to be, there may be at least 100 other points on your coach that require attention at some time to prevent a safety hazard or coach failure. A good preventive maintenance program: 1) identifies all of these points that you wish to include and 2) schedules attention to them at an optimum time that is neither too soon nor too late.

There are two basic components to a good preventive maintenance program. The first is to identify all the points on your particular coach that require attention and the optimum time frame when that attention should be given. The second is to develop a time frame for your preventive maintenance procedures. Since different items on the coach require attention at different intervals, you will need to group them on separate sheets based on optimum time. Your goal is to develop a separate sheet for each time frame with a list of procedures and checks that should be performed at that time.

Since the time schedule is probably the easiest to understand, we can start with that.

Scheduling of preventive maintenance can be done either chronologically or by mileage or a combination of both. Unfortunately, there is no one "best solution" that covers all coaches. A great deal depends on both type of use and miles operated. Moreover, there is no magic number of plateaus or sheets that should be drawn up. A simple preventive maintenance program usually has at least four or five distinct levels. Coach owners who use computers have been known to get very elaborate and go beyond this point, but keeping things as simple as possible is often better for most people. The trick is to determine what is best for you and your coach in performing the various procedures early enough to prevent failure but late enough so that you do not waste time and money.

Coming from the commercial end of the business and having relatively high annual mileage for a converted coach, I use a formula that is only slightly modified from a standard one used by many commercial operators. It includes only four plateaus or inspection times: each trip, 6,000 miles, 12,000 miles and 36,000 miles. In my case, my first inspection point is essentially chronological while the other three are based on mileage.

This procedure will probably work reasonably well for coach owners with relatively high annual mileage. At the exact opposite end of the spectrum are coaches that turn fewer miles. In that case you might want to look at setting your maintenance plateaus at 5,000, 10,000 and 30,000 miles. For even less mileage, a chronological arrangement might be more appropriate. If my coach were turning less than 12,000 miles annually, I would probably opt for trip, 6-month, annual and three-year inspections.

I happen to use the 6,000/12,000 mile plateaus because I like to change oil at 12,000 miles. This is really the extreme high end for oil changes but my mileage tends to be relatively easy and I use a very good grade of oil. If you want to change your oil at 10,000 miles then I suggest that you opt for the 5,000- and 10,000-mile plateaus. Or, you can design a more elaborate system for yourself. For example, Prevost Car recommends a slightly more elaborate preventive maintenance program with plateaus or inspection points at each trip, 5,000 miles (or twice a year), 10,000 miles (or once a year), 25,000 miles and 50,000 miles.

It should be noted that most preventive maintenance programs call for the various inspections or procedures to be cumulative. Let's use the trip, 5,000 mile, 10,000 mile and 30,000 mile program as an appropriate example. Before every trip you do the trip inspection. At 5,000, 15,000 and 25,000 miles you do the 5,000-mile inspection. At 10,000 and 20,000 miles you do both the 5,000-mile inspection and the 10,000-mile inspection. Finally, at 30,000 miles you do the 5,000-mile, the 10,000-mile and the 30,000-mile inspection. You then "set the clock back" to zero where 35,000 miles is treated as 5,000 miles and you start over again with only the 5,000-mile inspection.

If you were paying attention, you probably gathered that recommendations are that coaches that turn less miles should have their inspection points come earlier from the standpoint of miles but equal or slightly later from the standpoint of time. The major reason for this is that both time and mileage may be important factors. Coaches that turn more miles actually have an advantage from the standpoint of maintenance cost per mile operated.

Each of these plateaus, sheets or inspections are made up of a list of items or procedures to be done at that time. Unfortunately, it is nearly impossible to use standard lists because coaches and

---

12,000 Mile Preventive Maintenance

Coach Number _____   Coach Mileage _____

Complete ALL Items on 6,000-mile Inspection form
☐ 1. Completed ALL Items on 6,000-mile Inspection form.

Change Engine Oil
☐ 2. Change Engine Oil and Filter.
☐ 3. Run Engine. Check for Leaks. Check Engine Oil Level.
☐ 4. Service Engine Breather Filter.
☐ 5. Check Operation of Engine Stop and Fast Idle Cylinders. Clean and Lube if Required.
☐ 6. Service Engine Air Cleaners and Check Air Cleaner Connections.

Engine Fuel Filters
☐ 7. Change Engine Fuel Filters.

Lubrication/Grease/Oil
☐ 8. Lube Brake Treadle Roller and Check for Flat Spots.
☐ 9. Grease Upper Entrance Door Hinge.
☐ 10. Oil Lower Entrance Door Hinge.
☐ 11. Oil All Service Door Hinges.
☐ 12. Oil Radiator Shutters and Linkage.
☐ 13. Grease Angle Drive.
☐ 14. Grease Shift Lever Box.
☐ 15. Check and Lubricate Custom Coach House Air Conditioning Evaporator Blower Motors and Condenser Motors with 10 weight oil.

Check — Repair or Replace As Necessary
☐ 16. Check Block Heater Cord and Connections.
☐ 17. Ground Transmission Low Oil, Engine Low Oil and Hot Engine Senders and Check for Proper Dash Identification. Repair Senders or Indicators that are not Properly Working.
☐ 18. Run engine and A/C. Check for Engine Noises or A/C Noises.
☐ 19. Check A/C Mounts.
☐ 20. Clean Off Gradustat.
☐ 21. Check Accelerator Linkage for Binding and Full Travel. Adjust as Required.
☐ 22. Check Radiator Mounting and Fan Blades.
☐ 23. Check Hydraulic Fan Operation.
☐ 24. Check Fuel Tank for Wear and Mounting.
☐ 25. Apply Brakes and Check for Excessive Pressure Drop.
☐ 26. Check Alternator Output. Set to Specifications if Required.
☐ 27. Check Blower and Defroster Motors for Proper Operation.
☐ 28. Clean Differential Breather.

Fluids
☐ 29. Drain Oil from Air Cooled Alternators.
☐ 30. Fill Steering Gear.

Work Performed By: _____

Date: _____

Shown above is a good example of the format for a 12,000-mile inspection form. Note that each procedure is clearly shown and provided with a check box, and the form also provides for recording the mileage, date and person doing the work. Caution is advised in regard to the line items since each coach and coach owner is different and some of the items shown may not be proper for a given coach or owner under various circumstances.

owners are so different. These should be taken from: 1) your maintenance and service manuals, 2) past experience, and 3) common sense. Included are instructions to add or replace fluids, replace a part at a given time, adjust different items to an optimum position or setting, or simply check for wear or damage on some item and replace if necessary. They are then listed on the appropriate inspection sheet based upon the optimum time frame for them to be done. If you need help, check with the manufacturer of your coach, their service representative, or members of a converted coach group that you belong to.

Some people ask about the "normal" number of items or procedures involved in all the inspections of a comprehensive preventive maintenance program. This is really up to the coach owner since preventive maintenance programs are highly personal and reflect upon the needs of the coach and coach owner. Moreover, a great deal depends on how they are listed. Some people might simply list "grease coach" while others (like myself) actually list individual groups of zerk fittings to further insure completeness of the procedure. In any event, 50 or 60 items would probably represent a minimal program. However, there is no magic formula for the items you wish to include or exclude from your lists. The choice of items and your degree of intensity is entirely up to you. Many converted coach owners also include conversion items and systems on their preventive maintenance lists. In this case you can easily build your list as high as 200 items.

No two programs are ever exactly alike because of differences in make, model, usage and owner preference. However, there are some things that are relatively typical and worth mentioning.

Most trip inspections are primarily checks that look for problems. Typical are checks on fire extinguishers, all lights (interior, instrument panel and exterior), windows and glass, windshield wiper operation, leaking fluid or air lines, tire pressure and the usual fluid checks such as engine oil and coolant.

The semi-annual, 5,000-mile or 6,000-mile inspection usually contains the most items or procedures and generally includes a standard "grease job," a check on brake linings, a brake adjustment, a check on the less-obvious fluid levels around the coach such as power steering and hubs, plus a detailed check on various items or components such as belts and hoses. Any item found defective should either be replaced, adjusted or repaired immediately, or at least before the next time the coach departs. I might interject that I am personally a demon in regard to belts or hoses with any damage or substantial wear. Most are terribly inexpensive to replace at this point but could easily cause major problems if they fail on the road.

Either annually, at 10,000 miles or at 12,000 miles, most people change oil and oil filters. If you have not done it previously, fuel filters (usually two of them) should also be replaced at this point. Certain points that require lubrication or checking less often are done at this time.

The last inspection of the series usually comes every three years or at 30,000 miles or 36,000 miles depending on how your system is set up. Most coach owners pull their wheels at this time, check wheel bearings and refill the hubs to the proper level. Other typical items include changing automatic transmission and power steering fluid and filters.

Regardless of who does the work, we suggest that your actual forms be as easy to work with as possible. We use standard office-size paper (8½'' x 11'') with the name of the inspection clearly stated at the top. The various items and procedures are then listed and numbered sequentially. For convenience, I have them logically arranged into groups: lubrication, fluid levels, status checks, and actual replacement of items.

For some procedures, I include additional information since my criteria or requirements may be different than the next coach. For example, where a line calls for a check of tire pressure, I list my desired pressure at all three operating locations plus the spare. Where a line calls for the check of an oil level, I include the oil weight used if it can be considered non-standard. Hence, I show straight 40-weight oil for my engine but 15W40 for my auxiliary generator. Along the same line, I specifically indicate that I require a 50/50 mixture of anti-freeze and water for my coolant. There is also a notation on my form that the front bearing on the automatic transmission should not be lubricated since Allison manuals recommend against this. Finally, the form ends with a space for a date and signature for the individual doing the work.

The time required for these different preventive maintenance inspections will vary considerably depending on how many items you have listed, what they are, and what kind of tools and facilities are available. However, in general, the trip inspection can probably be done in 30 minutes. A good mechanic can do the semi-annual/5,000-mile/6,000-mile inspection in half a day. The three-year/30,000-mile/36,000-mile inspection could take most of two days.

A converted coach owner with the proper facilities and equipment could do virtually all of their own preventive maintenance. A pit would be helpful but not absolutely necessary. You can grease a coach with a hand grease gun but if you plan to do this, I would suggest that you invest in a small air compressor and a compressed air grease gun. Other than the simple trip inspection, many converted coach owners take their coach to a bus garage, bus repair shop or converted coach service facility for their more substantial preventive maintenance work and inspections. They not only have the proper tools and equipment but also keep spare parts and other supplies on hand.

Other Safety and Maintenance Notes

There are a few other items that fall within the range of safety or maintenance that are worthy of mention.

A very good idea that comes from the commercial end of the business is that *you should never start or move your coach without first walking entirely around it.* In addition to finding any obvious visual problems, getting into the habit of doing this walk-around will eventually pay for itself in saving damages. If you had forgotten that you had parked adjacent to a tree, curb, overhang or other hazard, this will bring it back to mind. In addition, the walk-around will also disclose whether you forgot to disconnect any of your lines or service hook ups.

Getting the best possible storage location for your coach helps a great deal from the standpoint of maintenance and reliability.

The best possible storage location is a heated garage. Next best, and what I use, is an unheated shed or pole barn, which is quite economical to put up if you are in a situation where space and ordinances permit. Next in line would be a simple carport type of overhead covering. Many converted coach owners also install a campground-type electrical outlet at their parking location. This allows them to turn on some heat in particularly cold weather or to run other electrical items on the coach without starting their engine or generator.

Finally, one last suggestion that I must pass along to you. The best thing for a coach is to be run. If possible, a coach should be started once a week and driven a few miles to allow the engine to warm up and the systems to become fully operational. However, this is probably difficult if not impossible for most converted coach owners.

Storage location can have a substantial impact on coach maintenance and reliability. The author's coach resides in this unheated pole barn with a gravel floor which at least protects it from the weather and possible vandalism. A campground-type electrical hook up permits heating the coach in cold weather or operating the electrical appliances without starting the engine or generator. LARRY PLACHNO.

One "old-timer" in the business suggested that if I cannot get out regularly with the coach, I should add one procedure to my preventive maintenance program: start and run the coach and major systems at least once each week. He suggested that this keeps the fluids moving, prevents gaskets from drying out, and may allow you to find problems. Since then I make a point of starting my coach once a week, usually on the weekends when I find time. I start the main engine and run the air pressure to the top, run the auxiliary generator for a few minutes, and (if temperatures permit) run both the coach and house air conditioning briefly. My experience is that this seems to help hold down maintenance costs in some areas, particularly in the air conditioning and the air system. Hence, I pass this on to you. It certainly won't hurt and may be a good addition to your own preventive maintenance program.

The author's coach out of its shed for an opportunity to run the engine and systems between trips. If your coach is not run regularly, it is recommended that it at least be started once each week to allow most of the systems to function. LARRY PLACHNO.

About the Author

Larry Plachno has been active in transportation most of his life. As a toddler, growing up on Chicago's north side, he expressed an interest in railroads. By age seven he was active in visiting different transportation facilities and collecting information. At the age of 19, Larry purchased his first bus and subsequently used it in conjunction with transportation activities including his operation of the last trolley buses in Columbus, Milwaukee and Des Moines.

He subsequently became active in commercial bus operations and worked for several companies in varying capacities including driver, driver trainer and safety supervisor, shop supervisor, dispatcher and both manager and contracted manager. Along with his wife Jackie, he owned and operated commuter coaches in the Chicago area and an intercity bus line in Wisconsin that ran a scheduled route as well as charters and tours.

Since 1977, Larry has served as the editor and publisher of *National Bus Trader*, the equipment magazine for intercity bus owners, both commercial and private. In spite of being a former private pilot, Larry has used coaches for most of his transportation needs. In the last decade, he has made the transition from commercial to private converted coaches through several steps including a party coach and an executive coach. His current coach is an MCI MC-8, converted new by Custom Coach Corp.

Unlike many converted coach owners, Larry uses his coach extensively and in all kinds of weather. His coach is frequently seen at both commercial and conversion bus shows throughout the country and often serves as a mobile office when gathering material for bus magazine articles. Jackie and Larry have five children, some of whom come along on various trips when the coach turns into somewhat of a family camper. He has been a member of the Family Motor Coach Association for several years and has attended virtually all of their summer conventions during the past dozen years. He is also a member of the Converted Coach Owners, an independent organization of private converted coach owners.